Juan the Chamula

Juan *the Chamula*

An Ethnological Re-creation of the Life of a Mexican Indian

BY RICARDO POZAS *Translated from the Spanish by Lysander Kemp*

UNIVERSITY OF CALIFORNIA PRESS

Berkeley, Los Angeles, London

University of California Press
Berkeley and Los Angeles, California

University of California Press, Ltd.
London, England

© *1962 by The Regents of the University of California*
ISBN 978-0-520-01027-7

Library of Congress Catalog Card Number: 62-16488

Originally published in Spanish as Juan Pérez Jolote:
Biografía de un Tzotzil *by Ricardo Pozas A., Fondo
de Cultura Económica, Mexico City, 1952; second
and third editions, 1959*

Illustrations by Alberto Beltrán

Printed in the United States of America

22 21 20 19 18
24 23 22 21 20 19 18

Translator's Note

A number of the Spanish and Tzotzil words used in the original of this book do not have adequate English equivalents, and therefore I have retained them in my translation. They appear in italics on first mention in the text, and are defined in the Glossary that begins on page 112. I have also retained the Spanish names of the saints mentioned; these are translated in the Glossary, but not italicized in the text.

Juan Pérez Jolote was first published in 1952 by the Fondo de Cultura Económica (Mexico City), which reprinted it in 1959 in both cloth and paperback editions. Although the author's primary purpose was not literary, his book has come to be considered one of the most effective treatments of Indian themes in contemporary Mexican literature.

A small section of this translation appeared in the *Evergreen Review*, Vol. 2, no. 7 (Winter, 1959), pp. 91–104.

Guadalajara, Mexico   LYSANDER KEMP

Contents

Introduction

Juan the Chamula is the biography of a man who reflects the culture of an indigenous Mexican group. That culture is undergoing profound changes because of its contacts with our own civilization.

The book describes the major social and economic relationships of the group to which the title character belongs, and should be considered as a small monograph on the culture of the Chamulas. It is not possible, in recounting the life of one man, to describe all the reactions of his group during a time of cultural change (much less so when the historical antecedents must be omitted); but an account of the most important components of his culture will make the narrative more understandable.

The title character is typical, in that he exemplifies the conduct of many men in his group. His life is not exceptional; on the contrary, it is perfectly normal of its kind, apart from the causes that sometimes induced him to leave his native village. For instance, his participation in the Mexican Revolution was merely an accidental episode, with no long-lasting effects on his personality.

Like all the men in his village, he lives under two economic systems, one of them Indian with traces of pre-Conquest organization, the other national and capitalistic. These two systems cannot be explained in any systematic way in a biographical narrative, and therefore it will be helpful to say something here about the differences between them.

The Chamulas are an Indian group of about 16,000 individuals who speak the Tzotzil language and live in rural settlements scattered in the highlands of San Cristóbal, near Ciudad de las Casas, in the state of Chiapas. Their center is the village of Chamula, which is dedicated to ceremonial functions; the political and religious authorities live in the village.

The Chamulas depend almost exclusively on the cultivation of corn, beans, and a few other vegetables for their daily food. The lands on which they raise them are arid and severely eroded. They use fertilizer but do not irrigate. Their only implements are the mattock and a long, pointed stick. Men and women have equal rights to the possession of properties. These rights derive from the traditional system of inheritance, and lead to excessive division of the land. The work in the fields is organized by families, with both men and women taking part. It is a coöperative method in which each person's share of the work is determined by his relationship to the family. There is little financial motive, since almost all the products are for the family's own use.

The economic system of the Chamulas has been strengthened by the adoption of certain non-Indian instruments and techniques, among them the use of mattocks, machetes, carding tools, and other iron implements; the cultivation of European plants, such as wheat and certain fruits and vegetables; the use of beasts of burden; the raising and utilizing of domesticated animals, especially the sheep, which provides wool for clothing and manure for fertilizer (the Chamulas do not eat its flesh, however); and the use of money in commercial transactions, which are an important complement to the economy.

However, these importations have not yet caused any fundamental changes. The Chamulas have learned the techniques used on the large Soconusco farms to which many of them hire themselves out, but these techniques cannot be adapted to a system in which both the work and the resulting products are distributed according to family relationships. The aridity of the lands, and their many subdivisions, also prevents any large-scale forms of cultivation.

In contrast to the system just described, the Chamulas have active economic relations with both Indian and non-Indian centers outside their community. They bring the products of their fields and their rudimentary industries—vegetables, eggs, charcoal, firewood, woolen sarapes, floor tiles, pottery, furniture, and other items—to Ciudad de las Casas to sell. They also travel to various Indian villages to sell woolen cloth, huaraches, sombreros, pottery, harps, guitars, and violins. In Ciudad de las Casas they purchase cotton cloth, cane liquor, sugar, salt, candles, copal resin, gunpowder, and other merchandise.

But their most important economic contacts are on the coffee farms of the Soconusco and Mariscala districts, where there is an almost constant demand for laborers. The farm agents advance sums of money to the Chamulas and other Indians who are seeking work, and these sums are then paid off by labor in the fields. Although this method assures that the contracted laborers will actually appear at the farms to work off their debts, it sometimes subjects the Indians to cheating and other abuses on the part of the farm managers. It is a necessary part of the Chamula economy, however, because it provides the money the Indian needs in order to marry or to fulfill certain of his social and religious obligations within his own culture.

The economy of the large farms is very different from that of the Chamulas, for it is based on the cultivation of a single crop, coffee, on great tracts of fertile, irrigated soil. Other differences are the use of machinery and a variety of implements; the hiring of men, women, and children from various cultural groups, often speaking distinct languages; and the marketing of the total production, in which the Indians never share.

Such work is not always available, however, and

the basic economy of the Chamulas still depends on the products of their own fields and domestic industries, with salaried labor outside the community remaining at most an important complement to it.

Although their economic system plays a determining role in their lives, a number of other factors must be considered in any attempt to understand the culture of the Chamulas. The most significant of these factors are:

A social structure with traces of exogamous patrilineal clans; a monogamous family, with authority vested in the father.

A religio-political structure with a large number of public posts and duties.

Education within the family, concerned almost exclusively with traditional precepts.

A system of common law practiced by the whole group and enforced by its own authorities.

A religion that mingles the worship of pagan deities and Roman Catholic saints, whose attributes are associated with the economic life of the community and the forces of nature, especially the sun.

The inter-relationship of these factors is in direct contrast to the limited contacts that have been established between the Chamulas and the outside world.

In conclusion, the typical Chamula—such as the subject of this biography—has the following personal and physical characteristics:

A strong constitution, which enables him to work long hours in the fields.

An aptitude for simple mechanical tasks, for which reason the Chamulas are preferred to non-Indian workers on the coffee farms.

An extremely individual concept of property.

A sense of collective unity limited to the ethnic group (the Chamulas treat Indians of other groups as strangers, and actively distrust anyone who is not Indian).

A desire to serve without remuneration in public offices, sometimes to acquire prestige, sometimes because of a sense of obligation to the community.

The use of cane liquor on all social, political, and religious occasions, in order to gratify and do honor to the living, the dead, and the gods, and to live in harmony with them.

A readiness to quarrel and fight when drunk.

A fear of reprisals by the living and the spirits of the dead.

A strong ethical sense, the most important values being: respect for human life (this is related to subjective concepts concerning the origin and cause of illnesses and death); honesty; truthfulness, to the point of surrendering to the authorities so that an innocent person will not be punished; and responsibility in paying debts, fulfilling obligations and keeping promises.

Finally, deep religious convictions.

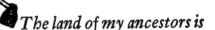*The land of my ancestors is* near the Gran Pueblo[1] in the *paraje* of Cuchulumtic. The house in which I was born hasn't changed. When my father died we divided up what he left us, and we had to take the house apart so that my brothers could have the poles and roof beams that belonged to them. But then I raised the house again in the same place, with new straw on the roof and mud to fill the chinks in the walls. The sheep pen has been moved all over the yard, to help the soil. The steam bath my mother used when I was born has been repaired, but it's still the same one. Everything is the same as it was when I was little. It hasn't changed at all. When I die and my spirit comes back here, it will find the same paths I walked when I was alive, and it will recognize my house.

I don't know when I was born. My parents never told me because they didn't know.

My name is Juan Pérez Jolote. Juan because I was

born on the day of the fiesta of San Juan, the patron saint of the village, and Pérez Jolote because that was my father's name. I don't know why our fore-fathers gave us the names of animals.[2]

From the time I was very small my father took me out to work in the fields. My father and mother would put me between them when they were work-ing together in the cornfield. I was so little I could hardly swing the hoe, and the earth was so hard and dry until the rains came that my knees would buckle and I couldn't break up the clods. This would infuriate my father, and he'd hit me with the handle of his hoe and say, "*Cabrón*, when are you ever go-ing to learn how to work?" Sometimes my mother defended me, but then he'd hit her too. He could always find some reason for punishing me. If he was making a palm-leaf sombrero and I was twisting the *maguey* fibers for sewing it together, and they broke, he'd yank my ears and shout, "Cabrón, how are you going to pay me for what you eat if you don't learn to work like me?"

He almost always took me along when he went to the mountain for firewood, and every time I went with him he hit me because I couldn't cut branches with the machete. He punished me so much that I began to think about running away from home.[3]

One Sunday when people were going by on the road from San Andrés[4] I stopped a Zinacanteco woman that I'd seen before. I was crying and I said to her, "Please, señora, take me home with you, because my father always beats me. Look at my head, here on the side, it's still bleeding. He hit me with the barrel of his shotgun."

"All right," the woman said, "come along." And she took me to her house in Nachij.[5]

A widow who owned fifty sheep lived nearby in a different paraje. As soon as she heard about me she came to ask if she could have me. "Why don't you give me this boy?" she said to the woman who brought me. "He hasn't got any father or mother, and I've got all those sheep and there isn't anyone to take care of them." Then the woman who brought me asked me, "Do you want to go farther away, where your father can't find you?" "Yes," I said. So I left with the widow, without knowing where she was taking me.

On the way she asked me if I was an orphan. "No," I said, "but my father always beats me." "I'm not going to beat you," she said. "I just want you to take care of my sheep." I walked behind her all the way, and we arrived at her house. I already knew how to take sheep into the mountains, so they could eat and drink, but I didn't know the Zinacanteco country or where to find good grass and water.

The next day she recommended me to other people who had flocks, so that I could take them to the mountainside to graze.

I don't remember how many months I stayed with the widow, but it wasn't very many because some other Zinacantecos, a husband and wife, came to ask for me. They wanted me to take care of their orchard. They gave the widow a bottle of *aguardiente* and she let me go.

My new job was to scare away the birds that were eating the pomegranates and the bananas. These people had two sons. They were very poor, and they earned their living by making turpentine and selling it in Chapilla.[6] The parents bought me a pair of huaraches. The two sons, who were bigger than me, took me out every day to work with them. One day they gave me a heavy can to carry, and when I tried to walk I fell down and spilled all the turpentine. They got angry and cut a switch and whipped me. I wanted to run away but those new huaraches wouldn't let me.

When I got back to the house I told the parents that their sons had whipped me.

"Why did you whip Juanito?" the father asked.

"Because he slipped in his new huaraches and spilled all the turpentine."

"Why didn't you carry it yourself? Can't you see that he's too little?"

"We made him carry it so he'll learn how to work."

"Besides," the other brother said, "it isn't true that we hit him."

I showed the marks left by the switch, and the woman said, "You're not going out with them any more. Then they won't hit you." After that I stayed at the house, carrying water and scaring the birds away.

That family didn't grow corn, and they didn't have any store of corn in the house. I don't understand how a family can live without having a cornfield, and I didn't know how they found the corn they needed.

One day they took me to the *tierra caliente* to look for corn. It was where the Zinacantecos have their cornfields. We found a man who had a great heap of dried ears. We all helped him with his work, some of us putting the ears in a net and beating them hard with sticks to free the kernels, others collecting the kernels and putting them in bags. The owner put me to work as if he were my *patrón*, and I spent the whole day in the field gathering the beans that were left on the ground. When I finished that, he had me chopping pumpkins with a machete, to get the seeds.

We worked for three days, and then the parents went home with their two sons, leaving me there to pay back what they still owed for the corn. A week later they returned, and I hoped they'd take me back with them to the *tierra fría*, but they went away again without me. I stayed with the owner of the corn, chopping pumpkins.

They came back again in another week for more corn, and I thought they were going to leave me there to pay it off. But that isn't what happened. They gave me a basket of snails[7] to carry and took me back to their house. I like it better in the tierra fría, because the bugs and mosquitoes don't let you sleep in the tierra caliente.

But then they took me to the tierra caliente again. This time the parents stayed home, and I went with the two sons. We arrived at the house of the man who owned the corn and they sold me to him for two hundredweights. We brought four animals with us and they loaded them up with the corn they were paid for me. Then they told me, "You stay here. We'll come for you next week." But they never came back.

There was a *ladino* who came there every day. He lived in an hacienda near Acala. He owned the land and the Zinacantecos paid him for using it.[8] One day, after the ladino and the Zinacanteco talked for a while, the farmer said to me, "Look, Juanito, from now on you stay here. You saw the animals loaded up with two hundredweights of corn. That was the payment I made for you, and you have to pay it back. But not to me. You know the ladino who comes here every day? You're going to pay it back to him. He came today to tell me he'd be back for you tomorrow, because he hasn't got any children, he and his wife are all alone."

The parents couldn't have known that their sons sold me. Or perhaps they were the ones who wanted me to be sold. I cried because I'd have to live so far away. The parents never hit me, or even scolded me, and I wanted to go back and live with them. I think they liked me, but they were poor and didn't have any cornfield. I cried for a long time because I couldn't go back. How could I go back, if they sold me so they could eat?

The man who bought me was named Locadio. The next morning at daybreak I heard his horse neighing, and then he talked with the Zinacanteco. He'd come to take me away. He put me up behind him on the horse and I went with him to his house.

He brought me to his wife and said to her, "Look, this is Juan, he's going to work for us . . . carry water, feed the pigs. Get him an old machete so he can chop up the pumpkins."

Don Locadio had a small dairy and he took me out there the first morning. He lit a fire, made some coffee, and gave me coffee with milk. He took me out to the dairy every day and we always drank raw milk. When I came back with him from the dairy, I chopped up the pumpkins, collected the seeds, and fed the pieces to the pigs.

While I was with Don Locadio the authorities learned that he had an orphan in his house, and told him that the Government was going to put me in a school. One morning two policemen arrived after I'd already come back from the dairy.

"Look, señor," they said, "the Mayor sent us because you've got an orphan here."

"Yes, he's here."

"Good. Bring him along now."

They took me to the Mayor, and he asked Don Locadio where he found me.

"A Zinacanteco had him. I went to where he was

working to ask for him, because I don't have any sons to take care of my animals. I had to pay two hundredweights of corn for him."

"All right," the Mayor said. "And how long has he been at your house?"

Don Locadio told him, and it was decided that I'd paid off what I cost him.

"And you," the Mayor asked me, "where are you from?"

"I'm a Chamula."

"Is your father alive?"

"Yes, he's alive."

"And your mother?"

"She's alive too."

"Then why were you living at this man's house?"

"Because my father always beat me and I ran away from home."

"I see," the Mayor said. "Then . . . your father and mother are still alive, and you aren't an orphan?"

"No, señor."

"The Governor thought you were an orphan, and I was ordered to send you to the school. But now that we know your father and mother are both alive, you'll have to go home."

They telephoned to Chamula by way of San Cristóbal, to have my father brought in by the *mayores* of the village. "What's your father's name?" the Mayor asked me.

"Sebastián Pérez Jolote."

They found my father and brought him to the Mayor's office in Chamula. They told him, "We got a telephone call saying that you have a runaway son and that he's in Acala. By order of the Government you'll have to go get him."

The next day he left to bring me back.

There were mangoes in Acala at that time of year. Before my father arrived I said to the Mayor, "I don't want to go home with my father. I'm afraid he'll kill me on the way." So when he arrived the Mayor told him, "Juan doesn't want to go with you because he's afraid you're going to kill him. But he'll go if his mother comes for him." My father went back to Chamula with a box of mangoes, and I stayed with the Mayor, waiting for my mother.

After about a week my father came back with my aunt, but I wouldn't leave. "Your mother didn't come," my father said, "but here's your aunt to take you home." I told them I wouldn't go with them, I'd stay in Acala. They went back without me, taking two boxes of mangoes they'd been given in Acala.

Two weeks later my father came back again, and this time I went with him, because he said, "I won't beat you any more. Let's go home, because your mother keeps crying about you."

When we got to the house, my mother said, "Have you come back, my son? I thought your father had killed you."

"No," I said, "he just used to hit me. You know how much he hit me."

Seven months had passed since I ran away from home. A week after I came back my father began beating me all over again and shouting what a trouble it'd been to find me.

I had an uncle who defended me, and he said, "You shouldn't hit the boy so much." My father told him, "It's none of your business! He's my son and I can kill him if I want to!"

One day my father asked for twelve pesos from one of the men that go around hiring people to work on big farms. When the day came for him to leave, they couldn't find him because he was out getting drunk, and they took me in his place to pay off the money he'd received. My uncle Marcos went with me. It took us four days.

There were plantations of cocoa and rubber on the farms. But I didn't work with the others, I just carried water for the foreman. The men were under contract for one month and they were paid twelve pesos. When they completed the month, other groups arrived at the farm to take their place. My uncle and I went back home.

When I arrived, my father asked, "Did you pay off what they gave me? You didn't leave anything owing?" He asked my uncle the same questions, and my uncle told him that everything was paid off. He added, "Look, don't hit your son any more. You didn't give him anything out of those twelve pesos. You didn't even buy him huaraches for the trip." "But if he doesn't obey me . . ." my father said.

A few days later he began to beat me again. He only hit me when he was sober. When he was drunk he never hit me.

My mother and I went out every day to bring in firewood from the mountain. One day the three of us went, and the animal we took with us wasn't well trained and wouldn't let itself be loaded up. I held onto the rope, but my mother couldn't handle the firewood she was trying to load. My father grabbed a stick and beat us. He hit my mother on the head and made her bleed. Then he beat the animal, and finally they got it loaded.

We went back to the paraje, but I kept on walking until I came to San Cristóbal. I knew the road because my father and mother often took me along when they went there to sell forage. I found a man who was looking for people to work on the Soconusco farms, and I asked him if he would hire me. I said I was running away because my father kept beating me. He said he'd be happy to take me, and we went to talk with the man who was advancing money. They asked me how much I wanted, and I said, whatever they wanted to advance me, but it shouldn't be much. I received twelve pesos.

Everything was cheap in those days, and I bought some bread, a bottle of aguardiente, a package of brown sugar, and a few peaches.

My parents had two houses, so I took the things I bought to the house that wasn't occupied, so they wouldn't see me. Then I asked one of my uncles to tell my mother to go to the other house to get the things I bought for her, but not to tell my father about it.

I took one of the wool *chamarros* out of the chest

where my mother kept them, and left seven pesos in its place. That left me three pesos for the trip, and I went to the farm.

Later on I learned that my mother had gone to the other house to see about her animals. I'd left the bottle of aguardiente under a little table, along with the bread and the peaches and the brown sugar, all of them in a basket. A cat got into the house during the night and ate the bread, and also tipped over the bottle so that the aguardiente all ran out drop by drop. When my mother got there and saw the things in the basket, she went to inspect the things in the chest and saw she was missing a chamarro, but she found the seven pesos.

She went back to my father and told him I'd run away to the farm. She said I'd taken a chamarro and left seven pesos in the chest. "Ah!" my father said. "So the cabrón ran away again! Why didn't you bring the money so we can go to San Andrés and drink *chicha*? . . . Go get them!" My mother returned to the other house for the seven pesos, and they went to San Andrés to spend them.

I arrived at the farm at Soconusco and earned ten centavos a day working with the young boys, because the men always worked apart from the boys. The men were paid according to how much work they did. My job was to weed the coffee plants.

The patrón and the foreman both liked me very much, and the foreman often sent me to the Tacaneco[9] country when his wife went back there, so she'd have somebody to go with her.

At the end of a year they were still giving me only ten centavos a day, because little by little they were taking out what they'd paid me in advance. After that they paid me according to how much I did, like the men. The first week I finished five jobs of work that paid fifty centavos each, so I earned

two and a half pesos. When I saw I was earning more I started to work harder, and the second week I finished six, and then seven the next, then eight, nine, ten, until finally I was doing eleven jobs in one week. The foreman noticed how I worked and gave me good jobs. I bought him cigarettes so he could smoke.

The first thing I bought myself was a pair of pants. When I had more money I bought other clothing, and later a pair of shoes, all from those women that go from farm to farm selling things on payday. The pants cost me eighty centavos; two shirts, sixty centavos each; my drawers, sixty centavos; the shoes, a peso and a half. I also bought some bandannas. My friends laughed and made fun of me when they saw I didn't dress like a Chamula any more. "Where did you come from?" they asked me. "We're all good friends, but now you're dressed like a ladino." I kept on working and bought a shotgun and then a pistol, so I could go out to the mountains on Sunday to shoot birds. After that I bought an accordion.

When my friends went back to Chamula after paying off the money that was advanced to them, they told my father that I knew how to work now, and that he should go to the farm to bring me back.

After I'd worked at the farm for three years I told myself: "If I go home without ever having sent my father any money, he won't let me in. I'd better send him something." I sold my pistol, my shotgun, and the accordion, and sent him twenty pesos by Mariano Méndez Aguilar.

Other gangs came and went, but Mariano never returned. Then some others who lived near my house arrived, and they told me my father wouldn't take the money. "But your son sent it to you," they told him. "I don't need any money from that cabrón!" he shouted. "I'm going to kill him!" I believed what they told me. He'd always beat me so much, I thought it must be true he was going to kill me.

I left the farm and changed my name, so that my father wouldn't find me if he came after me. I called myself José Pérez Jolote, and stopped being Juan Pérez Jolote. The farm where I'd been working was called the Premio. I went to the Lubeca farm, but I only worked there for five weeks. My friends from the Premio came to the Lubeca on Sundays to pass the day, and they said: "What are you doing here? Your father's going to find you, and he'll kill you!"

I was so afraid of my father that I left the Lubeca farm and went to the village of Huixtla. They were looking for people there to work on a farm called La Flor. I contracted to go, and when I got to La Flor the patrón told me: "I'm going to give you your meals and you'll sleep here next to the hen-house, so you can scare away the animals that try to steal the chickens at night." I slept there, and woke up when I heard a noise. Then I shouted so that the animals would run away. I worked at La Flor for about three months, and got to know three men from Comitán who had women with them to cook their meals. One of them asked me, "Are you going to keep on working here, José?" "Yes," I said. "Then don't eat over there in the kitchen. You can eat better here with my woman," he said.

The patrón gave out beans, corn, brown sugar, coffee, and laundry soap every week, and the woman who cooked my meals went to the patrón's house to get my share and her man's. I paid her five centavos a day to cook my meals.

The men from Comitán used to get drunk every payday. When they were drunk they exchanged their women among themselves, but the next day they were jealous.

"You, you cabrón!" one of them said. "You're screwing my wife."

"And you're screwing mine."

Then the third one came over. "You're screwing my woman, too."

And the fight began:

"Why don't we ask José Pérez if it isn't true?"

"He doesn't drink, and anyway I saw you, cabrón . . ."

They asked me if it was true.

"I don't know. . . . I don't sleep here, so I don't see what happens at night . . ."

"You mean you don't want to tell us."

That was right. I didn't want to tell them because I knew what would happen, but I'd seen the whole thing and the woman who cooked for me told me about it in the morning.

They fought with their machetes. The women and I were frightened and we just watched them. One of them was killed, and the other two and the three women ran away.

I didn't know what to do. "If I run away," I thought, "they'll say I killed him." So I stayed there, watching the blood run out of his wounds.

As soon as they knew that a man from Comitán had been killed, they went to tell the authorities in

Mapa.[10] The police came out to the farm to find out what happened, and they saw me there near the corpse.

"Who killed him?"

"I don't know."

"What do you mean, you don't know! You were right here with the rest of them. If you don't tell us we'll have to take you in."

"I don't know," I said. And without another word they fastened my hands with a rope and tied me to a post. They kept me tied up there while the people came in from the fields to see if I was the one who killed him.

The wives of the farm workers said, "The poor thing, who knows if he killed him or is just being made to suffer." They gave me some *pozole* to eat, but since I was tied up it was as if I didn't have any hands, so they fed me with theirs.

When the others came in, the women said, "José, you poor boy, they're going to take you away. Why don't you say who did it? Tell them how it began."

"How can I if I didn't see it?"

They took the dead man away, and they took me to Mapa as a prisoner and I slept there in the jail.

Early the next morning we went on to Tapa-chula and they put me in the jail there. I was a prisoner for eleven months and two weeks. I wove palm leaves and they paid me one centavo for each armful. A man from San Cristóbal named Procopio de la Rosa advised me not to sell the woven palm but to make sombreros out of it. "If you weave five armfuls, that's only five centavos. But if you'll make the brims of the sombreros I'll pay you three centavos apiece." I could finish two brims a day, and I earned six centavos.

They gave each prisoner fifteen centavos a day for his food. You could buy three tortillas with beans for five centavos, and that's what we ate every meal. If you wanted to drink coffee, you had to work to pay for it.

Don Procopio had five or six people working for him. When he saw what my work was like he began to bring me more and more bundles of woven palm for the sombreros. There was a light in my cell, and if I didn't feel sleepy I'd work at night, too. I could earn a little more that way, and have money to eat better.

The prisoners' wives could come into the jail, and their husbands would hang up sheets and chamarros so they could lie with them without being seen. Also, the guards would take all of us who didn't have women outside until they were finished.

Later on, Don Procopio told me, "I'm going to give you your palm from now on, so you can work on account." He was the one who sold the palm to everybody. He delivered the finished sombreros by the dozen to be sold outside. Then he taught me how to make sombreros that sold for a peso and a half.

Every Sunday the families of the prisoners came to the jail, and they ordered sombreros for their children and paid me forty or fifty centavos for each one.

Then I learned how to make fans for cooling yourself off when it's hot, and they'd pay me twenty or twenty-five centavos each. Some of them ordered more, and when they came back the next time I'd have them all made. I also learned how to make palm baskets, the kind with a handle.

I didn't suffer in jail because I learned how to make all these things. We had some prisoners there who said they were from Guatemala, and they didn't know how to weave palm or do anything useful. They just sat around waiting for their fifteen centavos a day so they could eat.

When they first put me in jail I could understand Spanish well enough but I couldn't pronounce the words. I learned how to make things by watching, because there wasn't anybody who knew how to speak my language, and little by little I began to speak Spanish.

While I was in jail we learned that the Government was in danger of losing because they killed the President. It was looking for people for the army so it could defend itself. Two of the prisoners wrote letters to the Government, and it told them that if they wanted to be soldiers they should put in a request. The rest of us didn't say anything, because we didn't know if we wanted to be soldiers or not, but the Government didn't accept just the two who wrote letters, it accepted everybody in the jail. Even the invalids got out along with the others.

The soldiers came for us at four in the morning, and the man in charge said, "All prisoners get their belongings together. You're all going to be free." But they took us to the station and put us into a boxcar, the kind that's used for cattle and bananas. The soldiers guarded us on all sides, and two of them stood at the door of the car, poking us with their pistols and saying, "Come on, get in."

I brought five new sombreros along with me to sell on the way. We arrived at San Jerónimo and they took us off the train and put us in a barracks. They took my sombreros away from me to start a fire so they could make coffee. They gave a close haircut to everyone who had long hair. They took our extra clothing away if we had any, and gave us coats with long sleeves.

The next day we went on toward Mexico City. I could hear them naming the different places we passed: Orizaba, Puebla . . . We arrived at San Antonio, where there was firewood. They took us out of the cars to rest, and built a fire so we could warm ourselves. It was the season when the corn is ripe. After we ate, they put us back in the cars and we went on until we reached the Mexico City station. They took us to the army post called La Canoa, and the next day they signed us up. They asked us if we were all Mexicans or if some of us were from Guatemala. Two of the Guatemalans told me, "They're going to ask us where we're from, and you ought to tell them that you're from Guatemala too. They'll let us go free when they find out we're from Guatemala, because Guatemala doesn't belong to Mexico. That way, you won't have to be a soldier."

The men in charge told us to form ranks, and then he asked, "Are there any Guatemalans here? Which ones are from Guatemala?"

"Here!" the Guatemalans said.

He told them to form a separate rank. I know I'm not from Guatemala, I'm a Chamula, from here, so I didn't like the advice they gave me, and stayed with the Mexicans. They let the Guatemalans go free and even gave them trainfare to go back to their homes. They also let the invalids go free, and just kept the rest of us.

They took us to a different barracks and made us take off all our clothes. Then they examined us. Those who had ringworm, like the men from Ixtapa or San Lucas,[11] weren't any use as soldiers because the Government didn't want them. It also didn't want anyone with boils or tumors. The only ones they kept were the ones with clean skins, and since I've always had a clean skin, without any sores, they didn't let me go free.

They began to pay wages to those of us who were left: twenty-five centavos a day and our meals. After a few days they gave each of us a pair of huaraches, and then a pair of shoes. Later they gave us kepis, and Mausers with wooden bullets, and now that we were in uniform they paid us fifty centavos a day and our meals.

The training started at four in the morning. The corporals, sergeants, lieutenants, and captains made us form ranks and learn how to march. At six o'clock we all drank coffee. There were a hundred and twenty-five of us, and we were from many different villages because there's a jail in every village. They called us the 89th Battalion.

A few days later they taught us how to handle our guns and how to shoot. We formed ranks, some of us in front and the rest behind, and when they shouted the command we had to throw ourselves flat on the ground. At other times they ordered some of us to kneel and the others to remain standing. They lined up some of our own men in front of us, and said, "This is the enemy. We're going to practice what you'll have to do in battle. Ready! Aim! Fire!" We pulled the triggers, there was a loud noise, and the little pieces of soft wood popped out of the Mausers. We were just training, so the bullets weren't real.

They said, "We're going to do it again. The first rank, prone position. The second rank, kneeling. The third rank, standing."

We did this by the count, taking three steps forward and then going back to our places. We repeated it every day, with our guns in our hands.

Finally they gave us real bullets, fifty to each man, and we began to earn a peso a day. After they gave us the real bullets we didn't fire any more, we just practiced the way they taught us before.

A little later we went out to fight Carranza. Before we left, a priest came to the post and they told us to form ranks. He stood up on a chair, we all knelt down, and he said, "Well, men, I'm here to tell you that we're going into battle tomorrow or the day after, because the enemy is getting close. When you're out there fighting, I don't want you to mention the devil or the demons. I just want you to repeat day and night the words I'm going to tell you: *Long live the Virgin of Guadalupe!* Because she's the patron saint of every Mexican, the Queen of Mexico, and she'll protect us against our enemies when we go into battle."

We left the next day. They loaded us into boxcars with our weapons, and told us we were going to Aguascalientes. We could hear artillery along the way, and when we looked out through the cracks we could see people running across the mountains. My comrades said, "It's going to be wonderful!" Some of them had guitars with them, and they played and sang because they were so happy.

We stopped in Aguascalientes, and then went on to Zacatecas. Then we just stayed there, because the train couldn't go any farther. They took us out of the cars and put us in a big house that was like a fort. We stayed there for several days. They got us up at four o'clock every morning and gave us a drink of aguardiente with gunpowder in it, to make us brave, and then gave us our breakfast. Those that had women with them were contented, they laughed and sang and played their guitars.

"We're doing all right," they said, "and tomorrow we're going to the fiesta."

The time came to go out to fight. There was a mountain near Zacatecas with a little hill in front of it, and the artillery faced the mountain. The artillerymen dug a cave near their guns and cooked their meals in it.

At nine in the morning we crossed a wide field to climb up the mountain, and while we were crossing it we heard the General shout, "Spread out!" The bugle blew and we scattered across the field. The enemy was up there on the top of the mountain, because the bullets came down at us from above. We started to shoot too, but since we couldn't see where they were, and they could get a good aim at us, a lot of our men were killed. The artillery was firing at the mountain, and some other soldiers ran forward and climbed up the mountain from the side, and the enemy retreated a little.

That night we had to bring in the wounded, without even having drunk any water all day. One of them said to me, "Take me back to the artillery positions. I can't walk. And bring my Mauser." I got him to the artillery. My throat began to hurt, and when I tried to drink some water it wouldn't go down. I couldn't eat anything, either, and I was deaf from the noise of the cannons.

They sent me to the post at Zacatecas, and then to Aguascalientes. I was in the hospital there for two days, and on the third day I was sent to the hospital in Mexico City, where I almost died from my earaches. First blood came out, then pus. I was in the hospital for several months, because they wouldn't let me leave until I was well again.

The people who were taking care of us began to say, "Who knows what'll happen to us, because they're going to come here to eat people, and we don't know what kind of people they like to eat."

The sick and wounded began to cry because they couldn't leave the hospital and run away, and those others were going to eat them. We heard it was the Carrancistas that were eating people.

A little later Carranza entered Mexico City. We could hear his troops go by in the street, shooting off their guns and shouting: "Long live Venustiano Carranza! Down with Victoriano Huerta! Death to Francisco Villa! Death to Emiliano Zapata!" They only cheered for Carranza. And we just looked at each other, there in the hospital, without being able to leave.

The next day the Carrancistas came to the hospital to visit the sick and wounded. They arrived with their officers, and after greeting us they asked, "How are you? What happened to you? Are you getting better? We're all friends now, that's why we've come to see you."

The men that had been crying spoke first: "They told us the Carrancistas eat people."

"What? . . . No, we're not cannibals."

"Then it isn't true that you're going to eat us?"

"Of course not!"

So the sick and wounded were happy. "Here's two pesos," the Carrancistas said, "and stop being afraid." They gave two pesos to each one of us.

I stayed in the hospital until I was cured. As soon as they let me go I went to Puebla and worked as a mason's helper, carrying lime and bricks. I also worked for some butchers, bringing the goats and sheep in from the haciendas to be slaughtered. They gave me my meals and a place to sleep, but they didn't pay me anything.

After two or three weeks I left Puebla and walked to Tehuacán de las Granadas. A butcher let me live in his house there. I'd already worked for butchers in Puebla, so I knew they were good people. I worked for him for five months.

The butcher's father used to go to the butcher shop at two in the morning to cut up the meat, and he always took me with him because he was deaf. When we went past the army post he couldn't hear the guard shout, "Who goes there!" and he was afraid they'd shoot him if he didn't answer. I had to answer, "Carranza!" and they'd let us go past without stopping us.

When we got to the shop he told me, "You can go back to sleep now, I'll wake you up when it's daylight." I went to sleep, and he cut the meat up into kilos, half-kilos and quarter-kilos. By the time it was daylight he had all the meat ready. He told me to get up, and he had our coffee made, one glass for him and another for me. Then the customers began coming, and he sold them what they pointed to, but if they asked him any questions I had to do the answering. When all the meat was sold he went home alone, because the guard could see him now and didn't shout, "Who goes there!" I stayed in the shop to sweep the floor and wash the table. Then I went back to the house to eat breakfast, and during the day I carried water and did errands and helped out with anything else that was necessary. I spent five months like that, going to the butcher shop with him every morning.

All they gave me was my clothing and my meals. I wanted to earn some money, so I went to the army post to talk with the captain. I said: "Captain, sir, I'd like to be a soldier."

"Good, good! What's your name?"

"José Pérez."

They gave me a shirt, a pair of trousers, and a kepis, and paid me a peso and a half.

When the old butcher found out I was a soldier, he came looking for me the next day. "Don't take him away from me," he begged the captain, "because I need him to help me. I've been good to him, too . . . I don't even criticize him. Ask him yourself."

"Is that true?" the captain asked me.

"Yes," I said. "I only left because I wanted to earn some money, but he's good to me and gives me my food and clothing."

"Well, if he feeds and clothes you and doesn't hit you or anything, you ought to go back with him. What more do you want? Good food, good clothes . . . he's practically your father. You've got a home now. We don't know when we'll be called out to fight. Maybe we'll all be killed. I feel sorry for the old man because he was crying when he came in here. Go back with him, hombre." The captain gave me five pesos, and I went back with the deaf man.

But I only stayed in his house for another week, because one day I met a woman who lived with one of my friends while we were fighting for Victoriano Huerta. She saw me in the street and said, "José, it's you! What are you doing here?"

"I'm just living here. Where's Daví?" [12]

"He was killed in the battle. I'm going back home. I'll take you with me if you want. I've got enough money to pay your fare."

I went with her to Oaxaca. She told me she was going to stop there and not go any farther, but she told me I could get home from there without any trouble. We arrived at Oaxaca in the train and she took me to her house to spend the night.

I left the next morning, to go home. I started asking the way to San Cristóbal de las Casas, but nobody could tell me. I must have asked a hundred people at least, but they all told me they didn't know. Finally I got tired of walking around the city, so I went to the army post to sign up. They asked me my name and wrote it down, and I was a Carrancista again.

After I'd been in Oaxaca for about a week they sent all the soldiers in the post to Mexico City, and I had to go with them. First they sent us out to Córdoba, and then to a little village where the Zapatistas had come in to rob the houses. We stayed there for six months, guarding the village, and that's where I first had a woman.

They assigned me to a lieutenant, and when I was off duty I went to the plaza to drink *pulque*. It was sold by an old woman with white hair, and one day she asked me, "Do you have a woman?"

"No, señora, I don't."

"Then why don't you find one? This village is full of pretty girls!"

"I know . . . but I don't know what to say to them."

"But you do want a woman?"

"Yes."

"And you've never had one?"

"No, señora, not yet."

"Let's go to my house."

"Good, let's go."

She gathered her things and took me to her house. She gave me something to eat, and after we finished eating she led me to her bed.

I went back to the barracks when we were all done. "Now that you know where my house is, you can come here whenever you want."

After that I went to the plaza every afternoon, and she always took me home with her. One day I asked the lieutenant to let me spend the night with my woman. He gave me permission. I went back to the plaza and waited for her to gather up her cups and the jar of pulque, and that night I stayed with her until the next day.

In the morning I returned to the post. The lieutenant asked me, "What about this woman of yours? Is she young?"

"No," I told him, "she's old, she has white hair."

After that night she used to come to the post when she wanted me to go home with her. She'd ask the maids who worked in the kitchen, "Is José in?"

"I don't know. Go in and look for him."

She'd go in, and as soon as I noticed her I'd

raise my hand to stop her, so she wouldn't speak to me in front of my friends. I was ashamed to have them see how old she was. I'd get up and go over to speak with her, and she'd say, "I'll be waiting for you tonight." And at night I'd go there.

At the end of six months they sent us to another village. The old woman who sold pulque stayed at home.

We went back to Córdoba and stayed there for a month, and then we went to Pachuca and stayed for two months. Next they sent us to Real del Monte, but we were only there for twenty days because the weather was too cold for us. We returned to Pachuca again and went out to another village, where the Villistas attacked us.

They entered the village at daybreak. We were all asleep, even the sentry, when the sound of gunfire woke us up. We all ran out and they started shooting at us. We had sixty-five men. Some of them were killed, some ran away, and twenty-five of us were taken prisoners by General Villa. They asked us why we'd become Carrancistas, and I said: "The Huertistas made us go with them, and when Carranza started winning we had to change sides."

"Where are you from?"

"I'm a Chamula."

The man who was questioning me, a lieutenant, turned to General Almazán and said, "These poor men were forced into service."

An old man with a big moustache said, "Well, what do they want to do now?"

I said, "I just want to be on your side."

"What about the rest of you?" they asked.

"Just what our friend said, to be on your side."

"All right. But look, if you try any tricks we'll shoot you."

"No, señor, we're telling you the truth."

"We'll see about that. We're going to send you straight into battle, to find out if you're really men."

They signed us up and gave us weapons and five pesos each, and that made us Villistas. But it wasn't true that they were going to send us straight into battle. A lieutenant named David León wanted me as his aide. "Look, José," he said, "if you like me, I'll ask to have you as my aide."

"Whatever you say, señor," I told him.

"Good, then, I'm going to ask the boss." He went to ask him, and the General said yes.

The troops went out in every direction, looking for food, but I stayed with the women. Every three or four days the women left the camp and went to some of the villages, and I went with them, guarding them and running errands. They gave me my meals, and fed me very well.

One day when I was watching the pack animals, one of the women that belonged to the soldiers came over and said, "Listen, José, let's go bathing in the river." She was really young, not like the woman who sold pulque, so I went with her. "Take off your clothes," she said. She was already undressed. We waded out into the river and she began to play by splashing water at me. After the third time I splashed back. She kept on splashing me, so I went over and embraced her, and that was when I knew what she was like and what she wanted. We came out of the water and went up onto the riverbank . . .

Afterwards we agreed that we would see each other on the mountainside. "We'll go there whenever you want," she said. So after I'd fed the animals I'd go there and she'd be waiting for me.

That's the way we lived, out in the fields and mountains where the animals could find fodder, until we arrived at an hacienda called Matamoros de la Azúcar. It had cane fields and a plant for making aguardiente, but there wasn't anybody there when we arrived because they'd all run away. They were afraid of us because they were Carrancistas.

We stayed there for a week, eating guavas, chewing sugar cane, and drinking plain water, without anything else to eat. Then we went to the village of Huajuapan de León and stayed six months. The people were waiting for us when we arrived. They were all Villistas and didn't run away from us.

The officers paid us all the money they had with them so we could buy what we needed, and when it ran out they began paying us with stamped slips of paper. These slips were only good in the village itself, and nobody else would accept them because they weren't worth anything. The leaders kept saying, "The money will get here in a day or two," but finally there wasn't anything left to eat in the village, and we couldn't buy anything outside because they wouldn't take the stamped slips.

General Almazán got us all together, privates and lieutenants and captains, and told us: "The Carrancistas have captured all the villages and haciendas. I'm leaving, because there aren't any more villages we can stay in. You can leave too, or stay here. Or if you want to join up with the Carranza forces in Tehuacán, you can do that."

We decided to go to Tehuacán, and left the village at night. We traveled across the mountains all night long, and when it was daylight we got some sleep and let the animals graze. The next night we started out again. We came to an hacienda near Tehuacán, and the leaders sent a note to the Carrancistas who were in the village. The note said that we wanted to join them, that we were a hundred and fifty Villastas who wanted to go over to Carranza. General Almazán had accompanied us as far as the hacienda, but when the messenger came back from Tehuacán with the answer, the General said to us: "Go ahead and give yourselves up, but I'm not going with you. If I did, they'd probably wring my neck." He left us that night, and in the morning we went on toward the village.

The Carrancistas came out to meet us, and we ran into them about a league outside Tehuacán. They all had their Mausers in their hands, aiming them at us, and we carried our own Mausers butt first to show we were surrendering. They marched us ahead of them to the barracks and took our rifles away from us at the gate, although they let us keep the rest of our things. Inside, they asked us where we'd been, and we told them about the different places we stayed at.

The next day they got us together and said: "Now that you've surrendered, what do you want to do? Do you want to be Carrancistas? If you don't, we'll let you go free, so you can go home and farm your lands."

I said, "I want to leave, I want to work in the fields."

"Where do you want to go?"

"To Veracruz," I said. Now that I could go free, I wanted to visit that town, and be a free man, not a soldier.

"You can go there, you can take the train. It won't cost you anything."

They gave me my ticket and twenty-five pesos, and above all they gave me my freedom.

I arrived in Veracruz and spent four days just walking around, without doing any work. Sometimes I'd sit on a bench in the garden to watch the people going by, and when the boys who give out handbills came along they always gave me one. I knew how to read by then, because I'd kept on asking for help from people who knew how. The lessons they gave us at the army post weren't clear enough, but I kept on asking and asking and finally I learned how. Then one day a man asked me if I wanted to work on a farm that was called Santa Fe.

I told him yes. They put me on a little steamboat that could only hold twelve passengers. It made a lot of trips carrying people out to the farm to work in the cane fields.

I worked there for nine months. They paid me two fifty and my meals. When I got tired of working there I went to a different farm called San Cristóbal, where I worked for three months in the cornfields. I didn't like it there either, so I came back home.

I had a hundred and forty pesos when I arrived in Tuxtla. I went over to one of the houses to ask if they had a place where I could sleep.

"Good afternoon, señora."

"Good afternoon."

"Do you have someplace I can sleep here?"

"Yes, of course. Won't you come on in?"

"No, I'll just stay right here." A friend of mine joined me, and we both slept there.

Two thieves got in while we were asleep, and I woke up and found that one of them was kneeling over me with his pistol aimed at my chest. "Let's see your pistol. What weapons have you got?" I told him I didn't have a pistol or a knife or anything. "Your money, then. Where is it, cabrón?" And he took my hundred and forty pesos. The other thief held a knife against my friend and robbed him of what he had.

In the morning I was very sad because I didn't have any money, not even a centavo, and couldn't buy anything to eat. I told the woman that the thieves had stolen my money.

"How much did you have?"

"A hundred and forty pesos."

"Oh, you poor thing!" she said, and gave me fifty centavos.

I was so unhappy that I fell sick. I had a headache and diarrhea and a pain in my stomach. After that I don't remember. The woman sent word to the police and told them an Indio was dying in her house. They came and took me to the hospital, and I stayed there six months.

When I was partly cured I began going to the plaza to bring back what they needed for the sick people, and they paid me a peso a day and my meals. I worked there for a month. They wouldn't let me go home because I still wasn't well enough. One day I said to the man who was in charge of us, "I want to leave now. I want to go home."

"Do you think you can make it?"

"I think so."

They gave me my thirty pesos and I started walking home. I stopped over in Ixtapa, and then I reached home from there in half a day.

I went into the house and greeted my father, but he didn't recognize me. I'd almost forgotten how to speak *Tzotzil*, and he couldn't understand what I was saying. He asked me who I was and where I came from.

"You still don't know me? I'm Juan!"

"What? . . . You're still alive! But if you're

Juan, where have you been? . . . I went to the farm twice to look for you."

"I left the farm and went to Mexico City to be a soldier." I was kneeling down as I said this.

"Did you really become a soldier?"

"Yes, papacito."

"Well, I'll be damned! But how come you didn't get killed?"

"Because God took care of me."

Then he called to my mother: "Come here and see your son Juan! The cabrón has come back to life!"

My mother came in and my father asked her, "Do you know who this is?"

I knelt down again. "I'm your Juan, mamacita."

My mother began to cry and said to my father, "Look at him, he's grown up! If you hadn't hit him so much, he wouldn't have run away from us."

My father said, "Well, he's back now, so that's that. Let's go inside."

They gave me a chair and I sat down and looked at them. I couldn't make any conversation because I'd forgotten too much of our language.

They called my brother Mateo and my sister Nicolasa to come see me. "Come here! It's Juan who ran away!"

My brother and sister came in to greet me, but I couldn't talk with them, all I could do was look at them. They didn't remember me, because they'd been so little when I left home.

"He's your older brother," my mother told them. "The one that ran away because his father kept beating him."

Then my sister said, "We thought you must be dead."

"No, thanks to God. He took care of me."

Some of the words I used were Tzotzil, but the rest were Spanish. Everybody laughed at me because I couldn't say things correctly in our language.

And I stayed here, I lived in my own village again. The first night I woke up when my father started blowing on the embers of the cooking fire. I was afraid he'd come over and wake me up by kicking me. But he didn't, because I was a man now! My mother got out of bed and gave him some water so he could wash his hands. She washed hers too, and began to grind the dough for the tortillas.

We all gathered around the fire to warm ourselves, and I watched the flames . . . how they surrounded the *comal* on which the tortillas were baking.

My father began to talk about the things that were being said in the paraje. He told us that the mayores took Mariano's wife, Rosa, to the village. That she'd been seen letting another man into her house while Mariano was out working. That she brought him there to sleep with her when Mariano was away at the farms.

My mother said, "These shameless women! No wonder their husbands beat them. Now that we've got our Juan here with us, please God he doesn't pick a bad wife."

While my mother was making the tortillas I remembered a lot of things I'd forgotten: my mother's dreams, the stories the old people like to tell, their joys and sorrows . . .

Three hours later the sky grew bright and the sun came up from behind the mountains. My mother put some coals into the clay incense burner and went out to greet the first rays of the sun. She dropped some pieces of copal into the burner, knelt down to kiss the ground, and begged the sun to protect us and give us health.

I returned to Chamula on the fourteenth of August, 1930. The next day was the fiesta of Santa Rosa, and my father said, "People aren't going to like the way you're dressed. You'd better change your clothes."

They took away my clothing and gave me a wool chamarro, and I fastened it at the waist with a leather belt, over my breeches and my shirt. Now I was a Chamula again.

But I felt strange in this dress. I was afraid to leave the house, I didn't want anybody to see me. I was so unhappy that I stayed home from the fiesta.

Those first days I worked around the house, doing whatever was needed. I went out for firewood every morning, and took care of the cornfield, and moved the sheep pen to another place.

I was very unhappy, because I didn't know how

to live like a Chamula. I asked myself, "Why did I come back to my village? What made me come back? I couldn't stand it here when I was little . . . And now everything seems strange, I can't talk with people and I've forgotten the customs . . . What am I going to do? I'm ashamed to dress like a Chamula, but they won't like it if I don't. I can't go out into the village because they'll look down on me, they'll talk about me . . ."

My father heard what they said after I arrived: "Look, there's that Juan. They say he's been out killing people. He's practically a ladino now."

I didn't want to stay in my village, but I couldn't leave again, either.

So I stayed around the house, working and listening to my mother speak our language. I was with her every day for a long time, just as if I were a little boy, and it was a pleasure to think that now I had a mother again. Little by little I began to feel contented when I sat by the fire.

Then it was time for the fiesta of San Mateo (Corpus Christi). The others all went to the village but I stayed home.

Later on, there was the fiesta of the Rosary, and I didn't go to that one either. I didn't want people to see me dressed like a Chamula without being able to talk with them.

But when the Day of the Dead came, I went to San Cristóbal with my father to bring back a jug of liquor. After that I wasn't afraid to leave the house with the others. It was the first fiesta I went to, and my father told me how to behave and what to do.

The preparations had to be made. There are special bowls and dishes for offering food to the souls of the dead, and these had to be taken out of the chest. They're kept in the chest all year and only taken out on this one day . . . the *setz* for the soup and the meat with cabbage, the *boch* for the unsweetened *atole*, and a little plate for the salt.

One of my brothers went to the village to ring the bell that belongs to our *barrio*. This was to call the souls. I went out to the graveyard with my father, to clear the weeds from our family's graves and to mark a little path in the direction of our house so the souls wouldn't get lost when they went for their offerings. The path began in the graveyard and ended with a sign that showed the entrance to our house. "My parents died here in this house," my father said, "and my father's parents also. The souls of your mother's parents will go over to the other house because they lived and died there."

In every house there was a table set with food for the souls. The table for our family's souls was spread with pine needles and wild orchids. Each soul was offered two pieces of meat in a cabbage soup, three *pilabil*, three *chenculbaj* and a *huacal* of *pajalul*. We all helped my mother prepare the meal and set it out on the table.

The only souls that arrived were those that had left things to my parents. The ones that hadn't left them anything weren't called to the house.

My mother called to the souls of her parents and grandparents, also the souls of my father's parents and grandparents: "Come and eat, come and taste the flavor of the food, come and enjoy the fragrance of what you eat."

That night they went to burn candles in the houses where other relatives had died. I stayed behind in the new house, which wasn't receiving any souls. We had a jug of aguardiente there. My brothers and sisters were with me and they went to sleep early.

There were candles in all the houses, and I'm sure the souls arrived to visit their families. My father came in with his relatives and friends to drink. After the first drinks they began to talk. One of the old men that came in with my father said, "How lonely *Chultotic* is! He still has his mother, *Chulmetic*, but his father is dead and never comes back to this world, not even his soul. He died a long time ago. The Virgin Chulmetic wept and wept when her lord died, and her son Chultotic said:

" 'Don't weep, mother. My father will return in three days. But if you keep on mourning him, he'll never come back.'

"Chulmetic wept and wept without listening to what her son told her, and the father of the sun never came back. If our mother Chulmetic hadn't wept so much, everybody who dies would return to this world in three days. That's why Chultotic goes to the *Olontic* every day, to see his father and to visit those who have died that day and can't come back again. Today is the only day their souls can come out to visit us.

"It's Chultotic's father who punishes the dead. If you used to steal or fight, he burns your hands. If you used to deceive your husband or wife and have a lover, he burns out your sins with a hot iron. If you murdered somebody, you're punished for your own sins and also for those of the man or woman you killed . . ."

They drank again and then went to another house where there was food set out for other souls. I thought the night would never end!

In the morning my brothers and sisters went to

bring back the dishes from the house where the souls had arrived, and at noon they passed out the food that the souls left behind.

I went to San Cristóbal on the third, very early in the morning, to ask the agent of El Escalón farm if he would advance me some money, and I was given fifty-four pesos. I came back home with the money and bought a pair of *caites* and a sombrero. I gave my father forty-nine pesos to keep for me, and told him: "If I work them off, good, they're ours. But if I don't like working at that farm, I'll quit and we'll return the money."

I left for El Escalón on the fifth. A foreman on horseback went with us. We were a big group. Some of them were drunk, others wanted to run away because they hadn't been paid what they were going to work off. A few of them were going to work off what their dead fathers still owed, and some were going to pay back the fines that the agent paid for them to the Mayor of San Cristóbal. The Mayor had thrown them in jail for walking in the street after dark.[13]

Three of them ran away. We arrived at the farm, and the work was so good that I stayed until I worked off everything they'd given me. I was there a little over a month, and as soon as I didn't owe anything I came home.

When I got back I found that my father had moved from the paraje and was living in the village of Chamula. He was first *gobernador* now. He spent my forty-nine pesos when he took office, to buy corn and *ocote* and a jug of liquor.

In February I went to his house in the village.

"Have you come back?" he asked me.

"Yes, papacito."

"Look, they named me gobernador, so I had to spend the money you left with me. I had to buy corn so I could live here in the village. But I'll pay you back later."

You can't govern the village or settle disputes or give the people justice without drinking aguardiente. The authorities gather in the town hall, and whenever the Mayor takes a drink, they drink too. If you want to make a complaint, or if you've been caught doing something wrong, you bring the authorities a litre or two of aguardiente, and the Mayor takes a drink and then the others drink. Separations, quarrels, land divisions, boundary disputes . . . everything is settled by drinking, by getting drunk.

These settlements are made almost anywhere: in the *cabildo*, in the first gobernador's house, in the plaza in front of the church. Each of the authorities who settles a case is given aguardiente in return. When my father was first gobernador, everybody who wanted justice would go to his house, along with the *alcaldes* and *regidores*. If the judgment was going to be made in the first alcalde's house, my father and the other authorities would go there. The people who had done wrong would bring them aguardiente and say: "Now that you know what I did, please pardon me and I won't do it again." The authorities would accept a bottle or two of liquor, and drink it. A little later somebody else would confess, and the authorities would scold him and receive more liquor. Others would come in to ask them for women, and they'd get even drunker. The secretary used to sell the aguardiente, and barrels of it arrived daily at the cabildo. My father got drunk every day, but I wasn't afraid of him any more. He told me: "Listen, Juanito, take a good look at the girls here, to see which one you like. We're here in the village now, and I'm an authority . . . so tell me which one and we'll ask for her."

"Good," I said, "but it'll have to be later because I haven't got any money."

"That doesn't matter. I spent the forty-nine pesos you left with me, so we'll sell the corn I've got here. There's still several bushels, and I bought it with your money."

"If you really would . . ."

I told him which woman I liked: she lived near our house and I watched her every day.

"All right, I'll ask for her . . . But you're sure you like her?"

"Yes! And nobody else except her!"

"But she's a Tuluc," [14] he said.

"So what? My name's Jolote, in Spanish."

He talked with my mother, and then they told me, "We're going to find out if they'll give her to us. You didn't grow up here and you haven't been back very long."

They went to her house with a bottle of liquor and they also brought me with them. When they arrived there they greeted her parents:

"Good afternoon, brother."

"Good afternoon, brother gobernador."

"Good afternoon, señora," my mother said.

"Good afternoon, señora gobernador," the mother replied. "What are you doing? Come in, come in. What do you want? What are you looking for?"

They went in and sat down.

"What can we do for you?"

"It's just that we . . . that we came to bother you for your daughter. You see, my son Juan came back a little while ago, and he wants to have a woman so he can live like the rest of us."

"But he didn't grow up here," they said. "We'll have to see what he says. Where is he?"

I was outside, waiting.

"He's outside."

"Tell him to come in so we can talk with him."

I went to the door.

"Good afternoon, Juan. Come in. What do you want? What do you need?"

I greeted the parents as I entered, and they gave me a chair to sit on.

"Tell me what you want," the father said. "Is it true, what your father and mother are saying?"

"Tell him why we're here," my father said. "And kneel down!"

I knelt down and said, "Yes, uncle and aunt, you know I don't have a woman, and I want to live like other people, I want to get married and have a woman of my own. I like your daughter and I'd like to marry her."

"But . . . do you know how to work? Because when you have a woman you have to support her."

"Yes, señor. Look at my hands. They're good and strong."

"All right. But there are lots of girls around here. Why don't you ask for one of the others? What about Petra Pérez Culish? It would be better for you to get married to her."

"She'd make a good wife, but I don't love her. The one I love is Dominga. I'll die if you don't let me have her. I know there are lots of other girls, but I don't want them. I just want to live with your daughter, if she'll accept me."

"But don't you see that you're like a stranger here because you didn't grow up among your own people? Maybe you just want to find out what my daughter's like, and then leave her when you go back where you came from."

"No, señor," I said. "It's true I didn't grow up here, but I swear to God that I've come back to stay. If your daughter loves me, you'll see how I keep my word. All I want is to live in our village and serve it the way the rest of you do."

They asked my parents, "Is it true, what this Juanito is saying?"

"He says it is," my father replied. "He says he's going to stay here and not go back."

And my mother added: "He keeps telling me every day, 'Ay, mamacita, I want to get married to that girl who's called Dominga.'"

Then the parents said, "Look, Juanito, it's the

custom here to marry a woman who works hard. Dominga doesn't know what work is, she doesn't know how to weave, she's nothing but a loafer. If you need a chamarro she won't be able to make it for you."

"That doesn't matter. If I need a chamarro I can buy one."

"What? Is he telling the truth?" the parents asked.

"It doesn't matter if your daughter's a loafer," my mother said, "because I can make Juan's chamarros for him."

I already knew how she worked, and my father and mother had seen her making chamarros to sell. Everybody knew that Dominga wasn't a loafer.

"Good," her parents said. "We'll try to decide."

"All right," my parents said, and gave them the litre of aguardiente.

They accepted it and called her in. "Dominga, come here. How many times has Juan talked with you?"

"No, papá!" she said. "He's never talked with me."

"Because if I find out you've been doing anything with Juan, I'm going to give you a beating."

"No, papacito, for the love of God! He's never talked with me ever, he just says, 'Hello, Dominga,' when he sees me, but I don't stop to talk with him."

"Well, he's come here now to tell us he wants to marry you. Do you want to? Would you like to be married to Juan? If you wouldn't, tell me the truth."

"But I don't understand what you're saying . . ."

"Look, I've accepted the bottle of liquor, so that means you're going to marry him. Go see your in-laws' house, to see how they behave, and if you don't like it, come back home. But not now, not until . . . until a month from now, because we have to talk with your aunts and uncles to find out about your in-laws."

"All right, papá."

"That's all I called you for. Go back to your work."

We started drinking the liquor. I served it, first to the girl's father, then to mine, then to the girl's mother, then to my mother, and finally to myself.

When the litre was finished, Dominga's father said, "Good, I'll be here when you come back next time."

We said goodbye and went home.

Five days later we came back to see what they were thinking, and to find out what the aunts and uncles had said about us.

"It's all right," they told us. "If he does what he promises, if he's going to live in the village and serve it, we'll give him our daughter."

We brought two litres of aguardiente this time, because I was sure by then that they'd give her to me.

They accepted the liquor and told me, "Don't imagine you're going to take your woman home right away. You'll have to wait till next month."

"All right," we said.

Then we all drank the liquor, and when it was

gone we went home. My father said, "It's certain now that you'll get her. We don't have any money, so let's sell that corn."

"Look, papá, we don't need to sell it. I'll go back and work at the farm."

I went to San Cristóbal again, to ask the agents for money, and they advanced me fifty-four pesos for three months' work. Now that I had money in my pocket, I just waited for the day that my in-laws set for the wedding.

The day arrived and I began to buy the things that were needed. I bought a peso and a half of bananas, a peso of oranges, two packets of brown sugar, six pesos of bread, four pesos of meat, a jug of aguardiente that cost me eight pesos, and four packs of cigarettes.

I had help in carrying these things because I got my brother Mateo, my younger brother Manuel, and my brother-in-law Marcos López Ventana. Their wives helped carry the basket of bread. My parents came too. I carried the jug of liquor.

We got there at six in the afternoon. We greeted the parents and they thanked us for the things we'd brought.

Dominga's father reckoned up everything, with an uncle and aunt to help him. They asked me what I paid for each item, and then what I paid for everything together. Once they knew how much money I'd spent, they began to serve the aguardiente. They drew off two litres and three-fourths of another. Now that they'd counted the expenses and had the aguardiente in the bottles, they told us, "Come in and sit down."

I was wearing a black chamarro, a shirt, breeches, and a new pair of caites.

They began to eat the supper they'd prepared, and after the first mouthfuls they said, "Now, Juan, serve us a drink of that liquor."

I served a drink to everybody who was in the house.

Dominga was wearing a skirt and a new *huipil*. She had scrubbed herself well, and had combed her hair very carefully.

After supper my relatives all went home and left me there alone. Before leaving they advised me against getting drunk, and told me to save my share of the liquor. They said to my father-in-law, "Don't make Juanito drink too much."

My father showed me how I ought to serve the liquor, and told me that in the morning I should get up at dawn and go to the mountain for firewood.

My woman's parents, grandparents, uncles, aunts, brothers, and sisters all remained in the house, and I stayed there with them.

They asked for more liquor, and this time they served it in bigger glasses, a full glass for each one of the men. When they gave me my glass, my father-in-law said, "Don't drink it, save it, because if I get drunk you'll have to take care of me, so I won't fall into the fire."

Dominga was sitting in a corner of the room, and when they served her her drink she poured it into a bottle. "Don't drink," she told me. "You have to take care of our papá."

"I won't if you won't," I answered.

She was holding a stick of burning ocote. She got up to put more wood on the fire every time it died down, and then went back to her corner. I sat with the bottle between my legs, watching what everybody did and listening to what was said.

"Look, Juan," my father-in-law said, "pour me out some more, because I feel like drinking. If you're not going to give me any more, why did you bring that jug?"

"Yes, *tata*, go ahead and drink," I told him, and filled his glass.

The other men in the house were Salvador Hernández Lampoy, my mother-in-law's brother; Domingo Heredia Mokojol, my woman's brother; and
my brothers-in-law Pascual Pérez Unintuluk, Andrés Pérez Unintuluk, and Agustín Pérez Unintuluk.
Each one of them had his wife with him, and I served
drinks to everybody. The women were saving their
shares now instead of drinking them, because they
wanted to stay sober and to offer their shares to their
husbands the next day.

Sometimes the men would talk while they sat there
drinking. "Well, our daughter's married. We'll see
how our son-in-law treats her." They couldn't speak
clearly by now, and one by one they fell off their
chairs and lay on the floor snoring. When all the
men were sound asleep, the women, who were all
sober, watched over their husbands.

My mother-in-law called me over and said,
"When your father-in-law asks for more liquor, we'll
tell him that it's all gone, that the jug is empty, even
though it isn't. They can drink the rest tomorrow."

A little later my father-in-law woke up. "Look,
Juanito . . . pour me another glass."

"Where's he going to get more?" my mother-in-
law asked him. "The jug's empty."

"All right. If there isn't any left . . . I'm going
to go to sleep." And he started snoring again.

My mother-in-law told me, "Stay seated there
and see if he asks for more."

Dominga was still in her corner, holding the stick
of burning ocote. The other women, her aunts and

grandmothers, were next to her, and I was on the other side of the room, with the men.

At daybreak I said to my in-laws, "Stay here, I'm going out to bring back some firewood."

"Good, son, go get the firewood, we're going to fix the things you brought." The women started to grind dough for the tortillas and to cook what I'd brought them.

I got back quite soon with the firewood. My father-in-law was awake now, asking for me. "Where's Juan? Where's my son?"

"He went out to get firewood. He'll be right back."

The breakfast was all ready. They'd boiled the fresh meat that I brought, along with some cabbage, and they'd also made a pot of coffee. The coffee was to drink afterwards while we ate the bread.

When I came back to the house my father-in-law asked me, "Have you come back, son?"

"Yes, papacito."

"Did you go out for firewood?"

"Yes, señor."

"Your share of the liquor last night . . . did you save it?"

"Yes, señor papacito. All of it. Would you like another drink?"

"Yes, son, that's why I've been waiting for you."

"I'll be very happy to give you one."

He told me to pour drinks for all the men that were sitting there, and told the women, "Serve breakfast while I'm having my drink."

I poured drinks for all the men. When they finished them, my woman brought the *bochilum* and offered water to the men, one by one, so they could wash their hands. Next my woman began to serve the meal, first to my father-in-law, then to the other men, finally to the women. The women served the tortillas they had made, and also a plate of salt. My mother-in-law said to my woman, "Look, daughter, the jug of liquor my son brought is empty, but here's a little more. Take it and see how much you have."

We added what she'd saved to the rest, and it made three litres. Dominga served some to her mother so she could drink it with the meal.

Before we started eating, my father-in-law said, "We're going to eat breakfast so you can go back home. You've all seen how I treated my son-in-law."

And they all answered, "That's right," "Yes, Uncle," "Yes, *banquil*, we all saw how you gave your daughter away."

"And we'll soon see how our son treats her," he said to his woman. "If our daughter behaves herself, good. But if they start fighting some day, and your daughter somes back home because she's angry at Juan, don't think I'm going to pay him back what he spent."

Then he said to me, "You've heard what we all said. Don't expect to get your money back if you should start beating my daughter."

"Don't worry, papacito. Don't worry, mamacita." I bowed to them and to each one of the relatives, for them to touch my head with their hands.[15] They did it, and that meant they accepted my show of respect.

The guests ate breakfast, returned the dishes, and went home. I was alone in the house with my woman and her parents. My father-in-law said to me, "Let's go out and work."

That first day we broke up the soil with hoes so as to plant corn. We came back to the house at noon to drink *pozol*.

"Are you here?" my father-in-law asked my woman.

"Yes, I'm here," Dominga said.

"Go fix the pozol, we want to drink some."

She served my father-in-law first, and her mother said to her, "Fix some for your husband too."

She obeyed her, and I drank it. When we finished

drinking the pozol we went back to work until dinnertime. Then we returned to the house for dinner. It was meat with cabbage soup and potatoes.

After dinner we went up to the mountain to cut firewood, and when we got back my father-in-law said, "You can rest now. If you want to see your father or your mother, go ahead."

I went to visit my parents.

"How did it go?" they asked me. "Were there any fights?"

"No," I said.

"Did you sleep?"

"No. We sat up all night."

"Good," my father said. "Now you'll find out what you've got to work at tomorrow, and when they'll send you back here with your woman. You've got to do whatever your father-in-law says."

"Yes, papá."

I arrived at the house a little late, and greeted my in-laws. "Good afternoon, papá. Good afternoon, mamá."

"Good afternoon, son, come in and sit down. We're sitting here getting warm."

I sat down by the fire until it was time for supper. After supper my father-in-law said, "Let's go to sleep, because we have to get up early for the firewood." Then he told Dominga, "Make the bed for your husband. Both of you go to bed now."

We slept in a bed that my father-in-law borrowed from his sister. My wife spread out the two *tasil* she wove for our marriage night, and also three chamarros to cover us. I lay down with my shirt and trousers on. She lay down beside me in her skirt and huipil, but she untied her sash. I began to caress her, and I asked her, "Do you love me the way I love you?"

"Yes, I love you."

Then I began to caress her breasts. "I want it," I said.

"No. My parents are still awake."

"So what? They did it too when they got married."

"Yes . . . but not now."

I felt tired and didn't have too much desire. Besides, I was afraid they were awake. And while I was caressing her I fell asleep.

Dominga woke up first. I felt her move when she started to get up.

"Are you going to get up now?"

"Yes," she said. "Mamá's already awake. It's almost daybreak."

Her father and mother were talking together. Dominga got out of bed and began to wash the *nixtamal* that had cooked while we were asleep.

The old woman also got up, and washed the *metate*. My wife had already lit the fire. A little later I got up, and the old man too. We took our axes and climbed up the mountainside to cut some firewood. On the way my father-in-law said to me, "When I married your mother-in-law I went out for firewood the same way. You'll both have to get used to getting up early, so you can save some money to buy livestock, because we're very poor. If she doesn't want to get up early, wake her up and tell her . . . or if you don't want to, just say so and I'll tell her she's got to get up earlier. I'm not going to keep you here any four days or more, you can take your wife home this afternoon. Some fathers make their sons-in-law stay for eight days, but I don't believe in it. You can take her home today."

I liked that, because now I could take her home to sleep with her.

Breakfast was ready when we got back with the firewood. After we ate, my father-in-law and I went out with our hoes to work in the cornfield. We drank pozol at about ten or eleven, and ate what we brought with us at one. Then we worked till four and went back to the house for supper. We had supper early because I was going to take my wife home. After supper my father-in-law said to his wife, "Look, Juan's leaving now, we're not going to make him stay. It's better for him to go home with his wife, to help his father with the work."

Then he said to my wife, "You, Dominga, take all your things. Your chamarros, the tasil . . . all your clothes."

We said goodbye to her parents. When we reached my house I said, "Hello, papá. Hello, mamá."

"Where are you going?"

"I've brought my wife, because my father-in-law said to."

Then my wife greeted them respectfully.

"Come in," my father said.

We went in, and since I had my own bed, Dominga put her chamarros on it after my mother told her, "This is your husband's bed. Shake it out and get it ready."

I also had my two tasil, my chamarros, my petate and my bolster. She made the bed.

My parents still hadn't eaten, so they said, "Come eat supper."

"No, we've already eaten. We'll have supper here tomorrow."

"Go to bed, then. What else can you do if you don't want to eat?"

We went to bed, and this time we took off our clothes and slept naked. She took off all her clothing without my telling her, and we got under the covers. She embraced me and I embraced her.

My parents finished their supper, made their bed and lay down to sleep. "You can sleep now," they said. "Goodnight."

"Goodnight," we answered, and they put out the light.

I didn't say anything to Dominga, and she gave herself to me without saying a word. We did it slowly, so as not to make any noise that would wake up my parents. That night I mounted her three times, once an hour.

In the morning I woke her up early and said, "It's daybreak."

My mother asked Dominga, "Is it daybreak?"

"Yes," she said. "I'm going to get up."

They both got up, also a sister of mine, and began to grind corn.

When the light was brighter, my mother said, "Get up now, it's time."

My father and I got up. We ate breakfast without going out for firewood, because we had enough in the house. After breakfast we went out to work in the cornfield.

I stayed in my father's house for four days, helping him with the work. Then I left for El Escalón farm, to pay back what they advanced me so I could get married.

The day I left, I told my wife, "I have to go pay back what I owe; the money I borrowed for our wedding. Make me about twenty *tostadas*, that's all, because I'm going to buy tortillas on the way."

"Don't you want anything else?"

"No. I'm going to leave you here with my parents, but you can visit yours if you want to, or even sleep there. I'm not going to be here, so it's all right if you do."

She made me enough tostadas for the trip, and I told her, "I'm going to leave you these twenty pesos, so you can buy what you want."

But she said, "You should leave them with your mother."

"Why should I? I've got a wife."

"She won't scold me?"

"No, take them."

She took the money, and I said to my mother, "Look, I'm going to give Dominga twenty pesos so she can buy what she wants. Fruit, or what you eat, or whatever she wants."

"That's all right. If you weren't married you'd leave them with me, but since you're married now, leave them with your wife."

It took me four days to walk to the farm, and when I got there they gave me tools to work in the fields. But I only worked in the fields for one day, because after that they sent me to help the mason who was working in the patio. I stayed there till I paid off the fifty-four pesos I borrowed to get married.

When I left the farm I had paid off everything I owed and had also earned fifteen pesos. I went to buy two measures of chile. They cost fifty centavos each.

I arrived home on the twenty-eighth of December. My wife wasn't there, she was at her parents' house. When I inquired about her, my mother said, "She's at home. She sleeps there, and just comes here during the day."

Later my wife heard I had arrived and came to see me. "So you're back?"

"Yes. I got back today."

"I . . . I slept at my papá's house, because I couldn't get to sleep all night here with you away."

"It's all right," I told her. "I'm not going to say anything."

"Do you want pozol?"

"Yes."

She stirred the pozol and gave it to me.

I was very tired from the trip and wanted to sleep. She made the bed for me and I lay down to rest. They left me alone and went out into the patio to spin and weave the wool. I slept all day. They woke me up at suppertime but I didn't want anything to eat. "You go ahead," I told them, "because I want to sleep."

After supper they went to bed, and Dominga came to my bed to sleep with me. She took off her clothes and began to embrace me, but I was still tired and she bothered me. I told her, "Leave me alone, I'm sleepy."

She lay still and I went back to sleep.

At daybreak I wasn't sleepy, so I woke her up with caresses, and mounted her once.

The sun rose and we got up and ate breakfast, and

then I went out with my father to bring back firewood. Later I went to my cornfield. Four of my relatives helped me work in it, and they ate their meals with us. When your relatives come to help you, you don't pay them anything, just feed them, because when they need help you have to go work in their fields.

My father showed me how to sow the corn before the rains came, by digging little holes and filling them with manure. We watered them for three days, and when the rains came the corn was already up.

I felt contented now, and I remembered a dream I had one night at the farm, that some men in black chamarros gave me a bag to carry. I told my father about the dream, and he said, "It means you're going to be given some kind of duty by the village government."

Once when I was talking with my wife I said, "I want to be an official. I'm going to ask for my duty as mayor."

"Ask for it, then. If they give it to you, then after we've served the village we'll be ex-mayores."

I liked the way she answered me, because I was anxious to be an official. Everyone who serves the village is respected for doing so, and I'd noticed how the past officials were greeted by the titles they had held.

Sometimes the officials would have to force people to accept their duties, because they would even run away from the alcaldes and mayores when it was time to enter the room where the oath is taken. The officials would catch them again and make them enter, to swear the oath at the foot of the cross. After they'd sworn they were contented, because then they were officials and that's important. I wanted my friends and relatives to help me when I went to that room, so that everyone would know I was going to be a mayor.

I know that some people can't accept their duties because they don't have enough corn to live in the village. One day the officials went by with a friend of mine. They were bringing him in to make him swear the oath and give him his duty. He told them he didn't have any corn and couldn't support himself, and suddenly he broke loose and ran away, with the officials chasing after him. I went out to defend him, and when they saw that he'd escaped they turned to me. "Look, this one'll make a good mayor." They took me to the room to give me my duty. After I swore the oath, they said, "You might be first mayor, we don't know yet. You don't have to spend anything to be a mayor, but if you want to do more for the village you can be first mayor, and that means some expenses."

I said, "Yes, sir, I want to be a mayor! That's why I grew up to be a man, that's why I'm here, to serve my village."

They got two bottles of aguardiente and took me to the house of the first alcalde. "Here's Juan Pérez Jolote. He wants to be a mayor."

"Where is he?" the first alcalde asked.

"Standing here."

The first alcalde looked at me and said, "Ah. Good. He'll be a good one for first mayor."

They opened the two bottles and we drank them. They gave me my staff of office and I went home. When I got there I said, "Dominga, are you here?"

"Yes."

"Dominga, now I've got what I wanted!"

"What?"

"First mayor! We're going to be first mayor!"

"How can you do it if you don't have any advance from the farm?"

"But I've already got my staff, and I swore the oath at the foot of the cross. We're going to do it somehow!"

Then I said to my father, "I'm an official now, but I don't know what to do."

"You don't have to do anything," he said. "Just cut enough firewood so you can live in the village. We'll get the relatives to help."

All the relatives helped me cut firewood when they knew I was going to be an official, and then they went with me to the house of the first mayor who was going to give me my duty. He told me what I had to spend and the things I'd have to do, and later I brought him some aguardiente.

My firewood was dry by the last day of the year, and my relatives took it to the house in the village where my father lived when he was an official.

On the thirtieth of December I put on caites, chamarro, shirt, trousers, and kerchief, all of them new.

The rods and staves have to be cleaned for the ceremony. The staves of the authorities of each barrio are washed at the house of the first alcalde of the barrio, so they'll be ready to be turned over to the new authorities. The silver handles are washed with warm water to clean off the grime and sweat.

They collected all the staves of the authorities in my barrio, placed a large gourd on the table, and put the clean staves in the gourd.

All the alcaldes and regidores and their wives had to bring a quarter of a litre of aguardiente.

The job of washing the staves is done by the clerks. They emptied aguardiente into the gourd so that it covered the ends of the staves, and then they scrubbed the ends of them with flowers and branches of camomile so that the aguardiente would take on the flavor and aroma of the flowers.

The clerks took up the staves one by one, first the staff of the first alcalde, next the staff of the second alcalde, and so on. They put salt on the silver handle, to clean it, and the salt fell into the gourd. Then they took a branch of camomile, dipped it in the aguardiente that was in the gourd, and rubbed the staff from the handle to the tip. They did the same thing to every one of the staves. When they finished doing that, they passed the gourd of aguardiente. The four alcaldes drank first, then the regidores, then the wives of the alcaldes, then the wives of the regidores, then the clerks, and finally the relatives of the authorities.

One of the clerks took a clean staff and placed it in the hands of the first alcalde, saying: "This staff is clean now. Take it, carry it with you, so that San Juan will be respected and will guard his village and

his people." The alcalde took it and said: "Little staff of San Juan, they have cleaned you well. Now help me in my duties, and watch over me and my family, my parents and my children and my wife. Go with me wherever I go."

The clerks handed the staves to all the officials, who said the same thing the first alcalde had said. Then each official held out his staff to everyone there, including those of us who were going to receive duties, so that we could kiss it.[16]

I had already washed my staff at home, with my wife and my father, because the mayores don't wash their staves with the other officials.

We received our duties on the thirty-first of December. The officials gathered in the plaza before sunrise. The mayores tied their staves into bundles and laid them in front of the officials. All the officials looked very fine. They were wearing black chamarros, and they held their staves under their arms, and their sombreros were decorated with colored ribbons.

The officials and their men walked to the room where the oath is taken. They covered a table with pine needles, spread handkerchiefs over it, and placed their staves on the handkerchiefs. The out-going Mayor stood in front of the table and told his men to go to the house of the new Mayor. They went to his house, carrying their staves, and when they arrived there they all knelt down and said: "Come, papacito. Come, mamacita. It is time for us to change, to give up our duties. God was with us, for nothing evil took place during this past year, and now we are ready to give you the staff and the oath." They stood up and drew closer together, then knelt down again to repeat what they had just said. Then they stood up and came forward and knelt down again at the door. The new Mayor was inside, and they repeated that they had come to get him. The Mayor said, "We will go to swear the oath now, and to take possession of the staff, for this is the day." He gave them aguardiente, they recited a prayer, and he and his *yajualtiquil* left the house.

The men who came for the new Mayor knelt down before him after every ten steps. They did this all the way to the room where the oath is taken. The out-going Mayor was waiting for them, and knelt in the doorway to greet the new Mayor when he arrived. Then he got up and the two of them went over to the table and stood on either side of it.

The out-going Mayor picked out his staff from the eleven staves on the table, and then made the sign of the cross with the handle of it, first on the new Mayor's forehead, then on his nose, then on his chin, and then on his breast, saying each time: "God *totic*, God *nichonil*, God the Holy Ghost."

And before giving him the staff, he said: "We are in good health on this sacred day, the thirty-first of December, 1931. In the names of our fathers and grandfathers, who rest in peace, you are going to swear that you will watch over our people in the same way that our ancestors watched over them. You are going to swear this at the feet of San Juan, and teach the cult of San Juan to your wife and children. The people will tend your cornfields so that you will have food. If you fail to serve our village well, you will fall sick. You must guard our people from harm every day of the year; you must stay here to watch over San Juan.

"Obey the ladino, because he gives the orders! He is the son of God, the son of heaven. His face is white and he wears shirts and trousers." [17]

"When you have to make a journey, when you have to leave here and can't speak directly to God, to San Juan, to our Holy Patron, you will speak to him in a cave or on a mountaintop. Even when you are far away, you will speak to him."

Then he gave the staff to the new Mayor and left the room.

All the people gathered around to present the new Mayor with gifts of money, because later on they might have to ask him a favor.

Then the alcaldes and regidores began to enter. All of them brought followers with them, from all the houses in the three barrios of my village. The followers knelt down in front of those who were going to receive duties.

When they brought me into the room where the oath is taken, it was already after dark. The first regidor gave me the oath. He touched me with his staff and said, "By the sign of the cross, you must climb the three mountains to see where the landmark of San Juan is, because that is what the ladino has ordered and he is almost our father. He will command us during the whole year, and if God is with us, first Mayor, all will go well during the year."

I served for a whole year, like the rest of the mayores, and that year there were four different secretaries. They sold candles, soap, and liquor in the office at the cabildo.

The mayores had to do everything the secretary ordered. Some of them had to go to San Cristóbal for liquor, others brought firewood to his house, others hauled water for his kitchen, others took care of his horses, others fed his chickens and pigs. I served as interpreter, because the secretary didn't know our language.

Everyone who came to the cabildo to make a complaint or ask for pardon had to bring a chicken for the secretary and some liquor for the Mayor. The person who was in the wrong bought the liquor from the secretary. If the Mayor, the gobernador, and the first alcalde saw that the offense was a serious one, they said, "You'll have to bring us four litres of aguardiente." Then the man who was being punished bought them from the secretary. If the offense was even more serious, they put him in jail. But the secretary would go to him and say, "Look, you know they're going to send you to Santo Domingo.[18] Give me five pesos and I'll let you out."

"Honestly, señor?"

The prisoner would send for his wife, and tell her, "Go get me five pesos, the secretary is going to let me out before the Mayor comes."

His wife would bring him the five pesos and he'd go free.

When the Mayor arrived, he wouldn't find the prisoner, and he'd ask the secretary, "Did you let him out?"

"No. Why? Isn't he there?"

"No."

"That cabrón! How could he have got out?"

When a woman wanted to make a complaint or

was brought in as an offender—one of those jealous wives who are always fighting with their husbands —then there'd be liquor for the officials and a woman for the secretary. One woman told the officials, "My husband's too jealous. I'm going away. I don't want to live with him any more." [19]

The husband said, "I don't want her to go. I'm a good provider. She has all the corn she needs, and I even bring her meat . . ." [20]

"I'm going back to my parents because I don't want to stay with him."

"You're not going anywhere!" the secretary shouted. "Take this cabrona to the room where they swear the oath!"

The mayores took her to the room and locked her up.

After the others left, the secretary said to me, "Well, first Mayor, we're going to have some good screwing tonight."

"No," I said, "I'm going home. I'll be back in the morning."

The next day, when the officials arrived, the secretary told them, "You can let her out now. We punished her enough last night, by locking her up all alone."

The officials let her out and she went free.

The women of her family asked her, "Weren't you frightened there in that room?"

"No," she said. "But the ladino came and told me, 'Look, María, if you'll let me come in I'll let you go free afterward.' 'All right, señor,' I said. He opened the door and I let him come in. Then he closed the door and grabbed me. 'I'll let you out right away,' he said when he was already on top of me. After he did what he wanted, he went out and locked the door."

When they let her out in the morning, she went back to her husband, because the authorities decided they should go on living together.

Another one of the secretaries had a big dog that slept in his room beside his bed. The dog ate there, out of a plate, and made his messes there too. Every day one of the mayores had to clean up the dog's messes and wash its plate.

Another secretary used to take the pulse of everyone who was accused of stealing. Then he'd say they were guilty and put them in jail, so he could fine them five or six pesos.

Another was a drunkard. He'd send the mayores to Chiapa de Corzo, where his family lived, with chickens, eggs, and fruit, or he'd send them to Tuxtla with a gift of chickens and eggs for the Governor.

You don't have to spend very much money when you're a mayor, but the mayores have to work harder than the other officials. They never get any rest, because they have to go out to the parajes to bring people in, and they have to wait on the secretary. But the year is soon over. They started to name the new officials, and my service to the village was coming to an end.

They sent me to the Romerillo paraje with some

other mayores, to leave a credential for the man who was going to be fourth regidor of the barrio of San Sebastián, which is my barrio. We got to his house at four o'clock in the morning. I knocked on the door and said, "Good morning, my friend!"

There wasn't a sound from inside.

I pushed the credential under the door and said in a loud voice, "I've left you your credential! You're going to be fourth regidor! We're going back to the village!"

While I was speaking I could hear the man getting up. I ran over to where the mayores were waiting. The man came out of his house stark naked, with his shotgun in his hands. He climbed up a tree and fired it into the air, shouting, "Cabrones, what are you doing?"

My companions answered him by firing their guns into the air, shouting, "Let's go! Run, run!"

We returned to the village shouting and playing our *cachos*, and we took a turn through Ciudad de las Casas while we were at it. When we got back we went to the house of the first alcalde to tell him what happened.

He said, "So you've come back, have you, mayores? But the credential you went out to deliver got back here before you." Then they gathered more men and returned to the house of the man who was going to be fourth regidor.

It wasn't the fourth regidor who brought the credential back to the village. He sent one of his daughters, and she left it with the daughter of the gobernador of my barrio. She took it to her father and said, "I don't know what this paper is." The gobernador took it to the first alcalde, who sent for a clerk to find out what it said. The clerk read it and told him it was the credential of the fourth regidor.

They appointed a delegation of fifteen men, but I wasn't one of them. The delegation left at four in the afternoon, and when they got to the paraje they waited until it was daybreak. Then they went to the house where the man's brother lived.

"Good morning, brother!"

"Good morning, my friend!" he answered from inside the house.

"We've brought you your brother's credential, and we're asking you to accept it because he's run away."

When he heard this, the brother was furious. The mayores told him it was a command from the village authorities. They tied him up as if he were a murderer; then they brought him back to the village and put him in jail.

As soon as the fugitive heard that they were going to force his brother to accept the duty, he came back to the village and went to the house of the first alcalde. He asid, "Let my brother out of jail. I'll accept my duty."

They let the brother go free, and they drank a jug of aguardiente at the house of the out-going fourth regidor. So the man was content to serve his village.

My year's service ended, and I surrendered my duty and went back to my house in the paraje. I owed fifteen pesos, and my father's death cost me another fifteen.

My father died from drinking too much, in September of the year I was a mayor. He got into the habit of drinking too much when he lived in the village as an official. This time he kept on drinking steadily for twenty days, and then he didn't want to drink any more because he was sick. He wouldn't eat anything, and he died.

My brother Manuel came in to the village to bring me the news. "Come home and see your father," he told me. "He's dead."

I went to the cabildo to ask permission from the secretary. "I want to go home," I said.

"Why?"

"Because my brother says my father has just died."

"Go ahead, then."

I went home with my wife and Manuel, and when we arrived we found my father already laid out. There were a lot of people in the house, including the musicians, who were playing their guitars and harps near where the body was. All my relatives started to cry when they saw me coming. "You've come," my mother said. "Your father's dead from drinking his liquor . . ."

"But there wasn't anything we could do," I told her, to comfort her. "It was his destiny."

There were some women grinding corn in the patio, and others were killing chickens to feed the people who had come for the funeral. My mother mended my father's clothes and chamarros, and fixed the things for the journey.[21]

My two brothers and my three sisters joined with me in paying for the coffin, and my brother Manuel and my brothers-in-law Mateo Patistán Acubal, Felipe Shilón Chau Chau, and Felipe Hernández Lampoy went to San Cristóbal to buy it. When they came back we put my father in the coffin. We all wept because he was leaving us.

The women put a table next to his coffin so he could eat. They set out a plate of chicken, a plate of tortillas, and a little dish of salt. After he'd been served, then the rest of us ate.

The sun was low in the sky when we started on the road to the graveyard. The spirits of men who die old get tired on the journey, and you have to give them plenty to drink. My aunt, María Pérez Jolote, gave my father some water every time we stopped to rest. They raised the lid and she dipped water out of the gourd with a laurel leaf and poured three little streams into his mouth.

When we got near the graveyard my Uncle Marcos took the net bag I was carrying, that had the things for the journey in it. He took out the basket that held the drinking gourd and took the bundles of food out of it to count them. There were three bundles of dry pozol and twelve bundles of tortillas. He raised the lid of the coffin and put the food at my father's right hand, under his black chamarro. "This is for you to eat on your journey," he said.

"Look out for it, don't let them take it away from you."[22]

Then he counted the three pesos that were in the basket and put them inside my father's shirt. He said, "This is so you can buy your chicha and limes and bananas, because we want you to eat well on the way. You can buy whatever your heart desires."

We came to the big cross at the graveyard and put the coffin down. The women all lit candles and began to weep beside the coffin, while the men helped us to dig the grave. The sun was about to enter the Olontic. You can't bury the dead until it enters, or their souls will stay on the earth.

My aunt put his other chamarros in the coffin, because all his clothing had to be buried with him.

After the sun went down there were still some red clouds in the sky, and we waited for them to turn dark. Then we lowered the coffin with the body of my dead father into the grave, and began to shovel in the dirt. The women stopped their crying and wailing, so that his soul wouldn't return. We filled the hole, packed down the earth, and washed our hands. It was night when we got back home.

I was sick also. An *ilol* came and took my pulse, and told me I was suffering from *komel*. "I'll come back tomorrow to cure you," he said. "Tell them to bring wax candles, tallow candles, copal resin, a litre of aguardiente, a rooster, and some flowers."

I knew this was how people were cured in our village, but I didn't understand why. That night my mother and my wife were talking about our troubles, and I heard them. Then I understood about the curing.

Each one of us has a *chulel*, which is an animal that lives in the mountains and represents us in every way. When the chulel is fat and contented, from eating well, its owner is healthy too. But when it can't find enough to eat in the woods, or when it's frightened or it falls into a canyon, then its owner gets sick.

The chulel of an ilol is wiser and more able, and that's why it takes care of our chuleles. The chulel of an ilol is called a *petome* or *saclome*. This duty of the petomes and saclomes, to take care of our chuleles, is given to them by Chultotic.

But they have to be coaxed to protect us. That's why the ilol drinks aguardiente when he's going to work a cure, because they like to drink.

Some of the chuleles in the mountains are stronger than ours, and they catch them and eat them. They're the *pukujes* and the *kibales*, which are the chuleles of the warlocks. If they catch a weak chulel, its owner gets sick, and if they eat it he dies.

The chulel of a warlock is called a *kibal*. When a kibal eats a chulel, the owner of the chulel dies.

The pukujes and kibales are fierce animals, the chuleles of men who do harm to others by eating their chuleles. That's why it's said that warlocks eat people. When a person is sick, that's because a pukuj tied up his chulel to eat it. The ilol has to give it the chulel of a rooster or a hen[23] so it'll untie it. He kills the rooster and the pukuj eats its chulel, and then it lets the sick man's chulel go free. When the chulel is untied, its owner gets well again.

The ilol came back the next day as he promised. Everything was ready in the house: the flowers, which they picked before sunrise, and the candles, the resin, the liquor, and the rooster.

He took my pulse again, and said, "What you're suffering from is anger. Now tell me if I'm not right." I told him I hadn't been fighting with anyone, unless I offended someone when I was drunk.

They put the flowers on the altar and hung up the rooster by the feet. The ilol lit the candles and dropped a piece of resin onto the hot coals in the incense burner.

He began to pray, begging the petomes to forgive me. He poured out a drink of aguardiente, splashing a little on the ground in front of where he was kneeling, and said: "Holy Earth, holy Heaven; Lord God, God the Son. Holy Earth, holy Heaven, holy Glory, take charge of me and represent me; see my work, see my struggles, see my sufferings. I place the tribute in your hands. In return for my incense and my candles, spirit of the Moon, virgin mother of Heaven, virgin mother of the Earth, and in the name of your first son, of your first glory, see your child oppressed in his spirit, in his chulel."

While he was praying he killed the rooster by twisting its neck, and suddenly I felt free. The ilol said my chulel had been mistreated and still wasn't well, but he told me that little by little I'd get my health back again.

That same year my son Lorenzo was born. Pascual Collazo Mechij, the midwife in my paraje, came to deliver him.

When it was time, Dominga knelt down on a petate and I sat down in front of her on a chair with my knees spread apart. She put her belly between them, while Pascuala waited for the baby from behind. I squeezed with my knees, and she strained and then she spread her legs wider so the baby could come out. Pascuala helped by tugging, and when she had it in her hands, then Dominga covered herself up to wait for the afterbirth. It came out, and Pascuala tied the cord with a piece of string and cut it off with the sheep shears. They gave Dominga a gourd of hot chile tea, and I went outside to bury the afterbirth near the house. I was very happy because the child was a son.

Three days later I fixed the steam bath for Dominga. I heated the stones with firewood, and put the water and the green boughs on top of them. Then I helped her to bathe.

A little later I went to San Cristóbal to ask for work. They advanced me seventy pesos and I came back to my paraje to get my cornfield ready. I cleared it and planted it and weeded it, and then I went to the Lubeca farm in August to work off the money they advanced me.

I didn't get back until after All Saints' Day.

When I got home I found my wife was in mourning for my father-in-law, who'd died in September.

When I returned from the farm they named me *fiscal* because I knew how to read. Andrés Tiro was fiscal that year, but since he didn't know how to read, he announced the wrong date for the fiesta of San Juan—the twenty-third of June instead of the twenty-fourth. When they discovered the mistake they put him in jail.

The fiscal has to know the dates of all the fiestas. I never make a mistake because I know how to read. When they come asking me about a certain date, I just look at the calendar and tell them, and after I tell them they give me a quarter of a litre of aguardiente.

They brought me in at New Year's to take the oath as fiscal. One of the oldest men in the village was my yajualtiquil. After I took the oath we went to the church and he taught me about the saints.

"This," he said, pointing to San Sebastián, "is the patron saint of shepherds. He sends out his sheep with the shepherd so he'll watch out for them. The shepherd is San Juan. If one of the sheep is lost, San Sebastián asks San Juan to replace it. When this happens, San Juan asks him, 'How much do I owe you for the sheep?'

"That's why the women dedicate their sheep to the care of San Sebastián on the evening before his fiesta. They also bring in grass and salt for him to bless, and give them to their sheep when they get sick.

"The people come in and say to him, 'San Se-bastián, take care of my sheep, don't let anything happen to them. I'm going to speak to your shep-herd.' They go over to San Juan and say, 'Señor shepherd, please take care of my sheep every day of the year. Watch over them wherever they go, wherever they eat grass, wherever they drink water.' You have to know these things," my yajualtiquil told me, "so you can answer correctly when the people ask about them."

Then he pointed to Santiago and said, "This is the patron saint of animals. The men and women who own mules or horses ask him to take care of them. They light candles to him on Friday because Friday is the day of the animals.

"This next is San Miguel, the patron saint of musicians. He's the chief of the harps and guitars, and the musicians pray to him because they have to play day and night at fiestas and funerals and he keeps them awake. They also ask him to take care of their wives so nothing will happen to them.

"And this is San Nicolás, the patron saint of chickens. He's carrying two trays full of corn to feed the chickens with.[24] But I don't know how San Nicolás can scatter the corn for them, because he's got a tray in both hands.

"This is San Jérmino.[25] He's the patron saint of the *curanderos*, because all the chuleles are in his care and he watches over all the souls. You can see he's got a lion at his feet. That lion is a man's chulel.

"This saint in the coffin is San Manuel. He's also called San Salvador or San Mateo. He watches over the people. They ask him to watch over them when they're at home or in their fields or on the road.

"This one on the cross is San Mateo again. He's showing us how he died on the cross, in order to teach us respect. They killed him because the Jews —the devils or pukujes—were eating a lot of people, and he gave his life to save us.

"Before San Manuel was born, the sun was as cold as the moon. The pukujes lived on the earth, eating people. The sun began to grow warm when the Holy Child was born. He's San Salvador, the son of the Virgin.

"The Virgin's relatives were pukujes—Jews. When she knew she was pregnant she said to San José: 'I'm going to have a child.' Her relatives knew that when the Holy Child was born he would bring light, and they made the Virgin go away. San José put her on a burro and they went to Bethlehem. The Christ Child, Jesus, was born there in a manger, on the straw. As soon as he was born the day grew bright and the sun began to give warmth. The pukujes ran away and hid in the mountains and ravines so the people wouldn't see them.

"If one of the pukujes comes out in the daytime when the sun is shining, it can't eat anybody because San Salvador is watching; because the sun is the eyes of God.

"Three days after he was born, the Holy Child didn't have anything to eat. San José was very unhappy and he asked the Virgin, 'Daughter, what are we going to eat?' Then the Child said, 'If you haven't got anything to eat, I'm going to start working.' Nobody knows where he got the tools, but he started to make a door from a log that somebody gave him. The log was too short to make a door, and San José said, 'The log's too short, it won't do.' The Child said, 'You watch, I'll make it do.' He took hold of the log and stretched it like a rope until it was as long as he needed it and even longer.

"When the people heard how he stretched that log, they came looking for him to kill him. He and San José and the Virgin had to cross the mountains and go from village to village in order to save themselves.

"In one village he planted a cornfield. There were a great many flies in that place, flies that bit. He said, 'I'm going to offer them supper, so they'll know I'm a hard worker.' Then he asked a carpenter to make him a cross. When the carpenter told San José, 'Here's the cross,' San José took it to the Savior. The Savior said to the Jews, 'Don't eat my children. That's why I'm here. Eat me instead.' And he was nailed to the cross.

"Before that, he went to see what the Olontic was like. Then, when he'd seen what it was like down there, he came back and was nailed to the cross. He had himself nailed to the cross so the people would remember that the devils—the pukujes—would be punished and wouldn't go on eating people.

"This next one is the patron saint of the church. His name is San Juan Evangelista. He was the first person to plant a cornfield. He was the first man in the world. He was born before Jesus Christ. He cleared the scrub off the mountains and taught the people to live the way they do today. At each fiesta the people ask him for good health so they can get their work done."

And that's how I learned about the saints that are in the church in my village.

Later they named me *hábito* for the fiesta of San Sebastián. Domingo López Sotot was hábito before that, but he died. The hábito has to shout a speech during Carnival, along with the *pasiones*.

Just before the fiesta began, they gave me the papers that the former hábito left when he died, but I couldn't understand them. They called the clerks in, but they couldn't understand them either. They all said they didn't know what that dead Christian had written down on the papers.

This was a bad thing for me because now I didn't have any speech. I felt very worried because I couldn't think of anything to say during the fiesta.

That night I went to bed and had a dream. I saw a man coming toward me but I don't know who he was; maybe he was God, but he looked a lot like Domingo de la Cruz Chato.[26] He came up close to me and spoke into my ear, and what he told me is what I say every year during Carnival. Everything he told me stayed in my ear, and I got up before dawn, lit the candle, and wrote it down. That's how I got a speech for the fiesta.

Then the fiesta began and all the people left the parajes. They all came in to the village for the grand fiesta.

The *mash*—men dressed in dark red coats, chamois trousers, caites, and conical hats made of monkey skin—came in along all the paths from the various parajes and went into all the houses in the village.

The *mesabil* came down from the mountains with their twig brooms. They formed large groups, by barrios, to sweep the plaza and the approach to the church, while the mash urged them on by whistling and dancing around them as they swept. More and more of the mesabil arrived, waving their brooms toward the north, south, east, and west. Everybody in the village had something to do. Some built pavilions covered with green branches, others cleaned the big pots for the atol, others brought firewood and water.

The *bajbín* arrived from each of the barrios, along with their groups of mash. They were dancing as they came, to the sound of guitars, flutes, drums, pottery drums, and the *chilón*. Every mash carried a flag on a long pole, and dipped his flag to the north, south, east, and west.

That night there was a fire in every house in the three barrios. The women made tortillas, the children shouted, and the musicians played their guitars, accordions, harps, trumpets, and gourd rattles for the dancers.

They killed a bull in each of the three barrios. This bull was in the house of the former pasión, and a great many women were busy there. The pasión sat on a bench in front of the big cross in his patio, wearing a black chamarro, new caites, and a sombrero decorated with many-colored ribbons. In front of him the mash shook their rattles and whistled the *bolonchón* as they danced for him. The women burned incense behind the cross, which was decorated with flowers and pine needles, and off at one side the musicians played their harps and guitars.

The *nichín* came in from their parajes, carrying the sacred box that held the silk ribbons and silver points for decorating the staves of the high authorities. Their mash came with them, carrying tall flags and lighting the way with ocote. They also had musicians with them, playing harps and guitars.

The day came when I had to speak to all the people of my village. All the important persons had gathered for the fiesta. Señora Nana María Cocorina[27] was in the room where the oaths are taken, along with her mash. So were the pasiones, with their mash and musicians, and the first alcaldes of each barrio, who were going to give out duties to the new officials and administer the oaths. Everybody ran to the plaza, and the arcade in front of the cabildo was so crowded that nobody could move a step. Inside, the pasiones were given their duties, and then it was the moment when I had to make my speech. I got up on the bench where the pasiones were sitting and took out my piece of paper.

I said: "Chamulas! Crazy February! On this day, the twentieth of February, 1932, the first soldier came to Mexico, came to Guatemala, came to Tuxtla, came to Chiapa, came to San Cristóbal. He came here with flags, with drums, with trumpets. Viva!"

Everybody shouted, "Viva-a-a!"

I could tell the people were enjoying it, and I continued. "The second soldier came to Mexico, came to Guatemala, came to Tuxtla, came to Chiapa, came to San Cristóbal. He came here with flags, with drums, with trumpets. Viva!"

"Viva-a-a!" they shouted again.

"The last soldier came to Mexico, came to Guatemala, came to Tuxtla, came to Chiapa, came to San Cristóbal. He came here with rockets, with cannons, with whistles, with bugles, with flags, with trumpets. Mariano Ortega and Juan Gutiérrez came here, and they went up into the mountains with their señorita, Nana María Cocorina, to have intercourse. After they'd had intercourse they came back down again, eating cakes and candies. Viva!"

"Viva-a-a-a!"

They all liked my speech and the fiesta became very merry. I didn't feel satisfied, because I thought my speech was too short, but they made me repeat it over and over again.

After I finished, the people left the arcade and

gathered behind their mash in three separate groups. I was with the people of my own barrio—San Sebastián—and we all went to the house of the new pasión of the San Juan barrio.

The mash ran around the plaza three times, dipping their flags to each one of the crosses. When they met the mash from another barrio they pounded the ends of their flagstaffs on the ground.

In the house of the new pasión of the San Juan barrio, everything was ready for the arrival of the important officials. Their bench had been placed next to the cross in the patio, and the table in front of it was loaded with bottles of liquor, water sweetened with brown sugar, baskets of small palm leaves, and various cups and jars. The little dishes of salt were on another long table, which was decorated with pine needles.

The bajbín were on the other side of the patio, with a drum, two pottery drums, the chilón, and a reed flute.

The pasiones arrived, each one with his yajualtiquil. All the members of the village government came with them and sat down in their proper places on the main bench. They brought bottles of liquor and *huacales* for the coffee, in baskets covered with napkins, and gave them to the high officials. Then they brought huacales of atol and blessed them and also said a prayer.

During the dance, the *chilonero* from each barrio put the chilón over each member of the government, and each member was given a flag at the same time. Then the chilonero and the official danced around the pottery drums of the bajbín. The official carried his flag as he danced, and the chilonero danced behind him, jingling the little bells on the chilón. The drums and flutes accompanied the dance. At the end, the chilonero lifted up the official and took a final turn around the drums, while the official waved his flag to the north, south, east, and west.

The Mayor and the old men who were with him blessed the liquor, and the palm leaves were passed out to everybody there. Then the liquor and the sweetened water were served; later, the coffee, atol, tamales, and soup. This last was made with meat and chiles. The yajualtiquil and the pasiones were always served first.

After the meal was over, the officials went back to the plaza, along with the mash, and all the people followed the mash as they ran around and around the plaza. After that they went to the houses of the other pasiones, but first they made me repeat my speech.

That night the out-going nichín arrived in the plaza, shooting off fireworks by the light of ocote torches. The musicians added to the noise with their drums, rattles, harps, guitars, and accordions. The nichín brought with them the boxes containing the sacred ornaments for the new nichín. The dancing and merrymaking lasted all night. I slept for a little while, but in the morning I had to repeat my speech again.

The plaza was still crowded with people in the morning. The high officials went to the houses of the former pasiones, where there was food and drink and dancing. I went with them, and whenever they asked me I shouted my speech for them.

The fiesta continued all day and all the next night. At three o'clock in the morning the mash were in the plaza with all the important people of the three barrios. They took three turns around the plaza, carrying ocote torches, while the music played and the fireworks exploded.

Then the people of the three barrios formed into groups to climb up to their crosses on the mountain. I went with the people of my barrio. We climbed up to the highest part because that's where the crosses are. The chilonero was there and so were the drummers with their pottery drums. The chilonero put the chilón on the people near him and then danced with them. We made big bonfires with our ocote torches, and the pasiones prayed and burned copal incense and cinnamon in front of the crosses. Then they took a drink, and when it was my turn they passed the bottle to me. It was a cold night and that drink tasted very good. I asked for a torch so I could see my piece of paper, and recited my speech.

"Crazy February! On this day, the twentieth of February, 1932, the day for climbing the three peaks of the three mountains, the day for going down to the three springs to eat the meat of a bull, on this day the first soldier came to Mexico, came to Guatemala . . ." and all the rest of it.

Next we went to the cross of the barrio of San Sebastián. There was dancing there also, and they burned incense and candles in front of the crosses. When the sun began to rise we went back down to the plaza, where we were joined by the people of the San Juan barrio. The dancing began again, this time in front of the church near the bottles of liquor. The air was full of noise and music: the jingling of the chilón, the shouts of the people, the sounds of the drums, the pottery drums, the rattles, the accordions, and harps and guitars. The plaza overflowed with people because everybody in the village was there.

Later we went to the spring, where the women were ready with baskets of tamales, bowls of soup and meat, pitchers of chicha, and jugs of liquor. Also, there were people from other villages selling liquor and other things. The high officials sat down at the table, and the rest fastened the flags to the cross that stood near the spring. The women washed their heads and feet beside the brook. All of us ate and drank and danced.

In the afternoon we went back to the plaza. They scattered handfuls of dry grass between the great crosses in the plaza and the entrance to the church, and then set it afire. When the whole path was in flames, all the pasiones—the new ones and the old ones—ran through the flames from the church entrance to the crosses, in order to purify themselves. The fire singed their legs, and the people shouted and shouted. They kept running back and forth in the flames until the grass was nothing but ashes.

The people spread out through the plaza and the mash ran around it with their flags. A bull had been tied up in one corner of the plaza, and the people gathered to look at it. They brought it into the middle of the plaza and a man got on it to ride it, holding the rope that was fastened around its body. But it turned out to be a coward and didn't want to buck. Then they brought in a different one, and everybody was happy because this one was really brave.

The pasiones went home, and I spoke to the people for the last time, to tell them the fiesta was over. They began to leave the village, and they were all so tired that in a little while the plaza was almost empty. I went to sleep.

The grand fiesta was over. The next day—the day after Carnival Tuesday—there was only one event, the visit to the house of Nana María Cocorina, where we danced and ate dried fish. That night the nichín watched over their ribbons and silver points. You could hear the sound of the fireworks that were shot off by those who were leaving the village. They lighted the way with ocote torches. Their mash went with them, carrying the tall flags, and so did their musicians, playing their harps and guitars. The officials also went home, along with their mash and musicians. All the people—the men, women, and children—left the village one after another. They returned to their parajes, worn out from so much merrymaking.

Then it was time to work. The men went out with their hoes to clear and plant their cornfields because the rainy season was coming. The women took their wool chamarros to the spring to wash them.

Back at the church, the mayordomos took the fiesta clothes off the saints and dressed them in work clothes. The musicians played their harps and guitars, but they were so tired that they played very softly.

I went home to my paraje. Some of the Zinacantecos who'd been to the fiesta were going the same way, and one of them told me he had a big book called "The New Alliance and the Origin of the World and of Mankind." He said he'd lend it to me so I could find a longer speech for Carnival. But I never saw him again, and I keep on repeating the same speech every year.

One night I dreamed that an uncle and aunt of mine came to visit me. They gave me two horses to take care of, also some hay to feed them.

Later I found out what the dream meant: my uncle was San Juan, my aunt was the Virgin of the Rosary, and the two horses belonged to the priest. It meant I was going to receive another duty, because afterwards I was made a sacristan.

The sacristans take care of the church, and their duty lasts their whole life.

I've served my village in many ways, and they keep on giving me duties. I was alférez of the Virgin of the Rosary, but I asked for that duty myself. The mayordomos and alférez can sell liquor, and that makes up for what they spend during the fiesta.

The man who appointed me alférez gave me fifteen pesos so I could begin to sell liquor. I bought a large jug, and every Sunday I went to the plaza to sell it. All my friends offered me a drink when they bought aguardiente from me, and I got drunk again and again.

I couldn't help drinking. I was alférez of the Virgin of the Rosary, and since she's a woman, that made me a woman too, and I was invited to drink with all those who take care of the saints that are men.

After I finished my duty as alférez, the village secretary called me in and said, "The President of Mexico wants all the Chamulas to learn how to read, but first they have to learn how to speak Spanish. The government wants you to be a Spanish teacher, and it'll pay you fifty pesos a month."

"If it's an order from the Mexican government," I said, "then I'll do it."

The Government appointed twelve teachers to teach Spanish to the people in our parajes. I had thirty students in Cuchulumtic and I taught them some Spanish words and the alphabet so they'd know how to read. After three years the campaign ended and we weren't teachers any more. There aren't any classes now, so the people who want to learn Spanish go to the drugstore in San Cristóbal and buy a certain kind of oil. They say this oil helps you to learn Spanish.

Now they've given me another duty: I'm the alférez of San Juan. I sell liquor here in my house, two big jugs of it every day. When I can't go out to buy it, my son Lorenzo goes. One day the inspectors took one of my jugs away from me because I didn't buy it where I should have. There are two places that make aguardiente in San Cristóbal, and the owners have divided the villages between them: one of them sells it to the Chamulas and the Zinacantecos, the other sells it to the other villages.

There are lots of other villages, so the other owner is the richest man in San Cristóbal and can pay to have inspectors. They go from house to house with their pistols and Mausers, and if they find any contraband liquor or any liquor from the wrong store, they either kill the man or take him off to jail. Nobody else can make or sell aguardiente, because they've arranged it that way with the Government.[28]

My friends come to my house every day to buy aguardiente, and they always give me a drink. My son Lorenzo and my wife Dominga keep telling me to stop drinking, but I can't. Sometimes I don't eat anything all day long. That's how my father died, from not eating.

But I don't want to die. I want to live.

Notes

1 The "Great Village," that is, Chamula.
2 *Jolote* is a regional form of *guajolote*, "turkey." The custom of giving names derived from those of animals, plants, and objects dates from before the Conquest.
3 This is exceptional: the Chamulas usually treat their children well, and rarely strike them, and the children rarely run away from home.
4 Indian village near Chamula. Its present name is Larráinzar.
5 Paraje near Chamula.
6 Village in the lowlands south of Chamula.
7 River snails, *Subulinidal opeas Sp.*, considered a delicacy by the Chamulas.
8 The Zinacantecos rent land in the valley of the Rio Grande to raise corn; the Chamulas work for them as peons.
9 Indigenous group living near the Tacaná volcano.
10 Village in the lowlands south of Chamula.
11 Village in the lowlands south of Chamula.

12 David. In Mexico the final "d" is often not pro-
nounced; for example, *usté* for *usted*, "you."

13 The Mayor of San Cristóbal, by agreement with the
agents, ordered the arrest of any Indians found in
the streets after seven o'clock at night. The agents
paid the fines and thus obtained workers for the
farm.

14 Tzotzil word for *guajolote* or *jolote,* both of which
mean "turkey." There are still vestiges of exogamous clans among the Chamulas, one of the evi-
dences being the prohibition of marriage between
persons of the same name.

15 It is the custom among the Chamulas to show respect
for one's elders, or for persons of higher station,
by bowing one's head.

16 The village of Chamula has two governments, although this is contrary to the provisions of the
Mexican Constitution; the cause is the disparity
between the political organization of the country
as a whole and the internal political organization
of the Chamulas. One of the governments, the regional, comprising fifty-one officials from the three
barrios, has no legal standing; its functions are
closely linked to the religious activities of the community. The other, the constitutional, consists of
a mayor, two aldermen, two substitute aldermen,
and a recorder. The ceremony described by Juan
pertains to the regional government.

17 Although the secretary of the village government
should be appointed by the mayor, he is imposed
here by higher, non-Indian authorities, and is himself non-Indian (ladino). He wields great influ-
ence, overruling all the other village officials.

18 The prison in San Cristóbal de las Casas.

19 In cases of separation among the Chamulas, the woman usually takes the initiative.

20 Meat is considered the finest of gifts by the Chamulas.

21 The Chamulas believe that the dead have to walk a long distance and to cross a lake infested with dogs, one of which serves the dead as a mount to take him from one shore to the other.

22 When the dead arrive in the afterworld, all the souls beg them to give them what they have brought.

23 Animals also have *chuleles*, which are other animals.

24 A wooden figure, without hands, apparently representing San Antonio; its long wide sleeves resemble trays.

25 San Jerónimo.

26 A group of old men called *principales* is consulted whenever an important matter comes up in the village. Domingo de la Cruz Chato was a member of the group.

27 A man, dressed as a woman, who carries a copal incense burner and accompanies the important religious officials.

28 These exclusive rights to production and sales were granted by the state government, which received high tax payments in return.

Glossary

aguardiente: a strong, clear liquor made from sugar cane.

alcalde: an important village official, with both political and religious duties.

alférez: a religious functionary assigned to care for one of the figures of the saints in the village church.

atol, atole: a thick beverage made with finely ground corn meal and water.

bajbín: a religious functionary who plays a pottery drum, that is, a clay pot with a skin stretched over its mouth as a drumhead.

banquil: elder brother.

barrio: sector, neighborhood, quarter.

boch: a gourd used as a drinking vessel.

bochilum: a clay finger bowl.

bolonchón: a song played and whistled by the Chamulas; literally, "tiger" (i.e., "jaguar").

cabildo: town hall.

cabrón: literally, "he-goat"; an offensive epithet roughly equivalent to "bastard" or "son of a bitch."

cabrona: an offensive epithet roughly equivalent to "bitch."

cacho: bull's horn.

caites: huaraches of a special kind, with tall heel-pieces and a thong between the first two toes.

chamarro: a woolen sarape woven on looms of pre-Conquest design; it is usually somewhat shorter than the sarapes worn elsewhere in Mexico.

chenculbaj: tamales containing mashed beans instead of meat.

chicha: a drink made from fermented sugar cane.

chilón: a jaguar skin to which a number of small bells have been attached.

chilonero: the man in charge of the *chilón* during the Carnival festivities.

chulel: the soul embodied in an animal.

Chulmetic: the sacred señora or lady, that is, the Moon.

Chuloltic: the sacred señor or lord, that is, the Sun.

comal: a round, flat pottery plate for baking tortillas.

curandero: healer.

fiscal: a religious functionary whose main duty is to announce the correct dates of the fiestas.

gobernador: a village official more important than a *mayor* but less important than an *alcalde.*

hábito: the person designated to deliver a speech during the Carnival festivities.

huacal: a gourd used as a drinking vessel.

huipil: a long, sleeveless cotton blouse.

ilol: healer (*curandero*).

kibal: see *pukuj.*

komel: sickness caused by fear or surprise.

ladino: a person who is not Indian.

maguey: agave.

mash: persons who accompany the officials during the Carnival festivities; their functions are both humorous and solemn; literally the word means "monkeys."

mayor: the least important of the village officials.

mayordomo: a caretaker in the village church.

mesabil: persons who sweep the plaza during Carnival.

metate: the stone platform or table on which the *nixtamal* is ground for the making of tortillas, tamales, and the like.

nichín: religious functionaries who take charge of the sacred objects during Carnival.

nichonil: God the Son.

nixtamal: parboiled corn to be ground for making tortillas.

ocote: a resinous wood used as candles and torches.

Olontic: the after-world.

pajalul: unsweetened *atole*.

paraje: rural sector.

pasión: religious functionary during the Carnival fiesta; each of the three *barrios* has its own *pasión*.

patrón: patron, boss, owner.

petome: a female chulel.

petate: woven rush mat.

pilabil: tamales containing whole beans.

pozol: a beverage prepared from twice-cooked corn which is ground to a powder and mixed with water when wanted.

pozole: corn dough thinned with water.

pukuj: the *chulel* of a warlock; a demon; a Jew.

pulque: a kind of beer made from the fermented juices of a certain type of agave plant.

regidor: a village official of middle rank.

saclome: a male *chulel*.

San Cristóbal: St. Christopher.

San Jerónimo: St. Jerome.

San José: St. Joseph.

San Juan: St. John.

San Juan Evangelista: St. John the Evangelist.

San Manuel: St. Manuel.

San Mateo: St. Matthew.

San Miguel: St. Michael.

San Nicolás: St. Nicholas.

San Salvador: the Savior.

San Sebastián: St. Sebastian.

Santiago: St. James.

setz: deep dishes made of glazed clay.

tasil: a sort of wool blanket woven on a loom of pre-Conquest design.

tata: literally, "daddy," but in Mexico it is applied not only to one's father but also to one's father-in-law, the priests, Jesus Christ, and God.

tierra caliente: "hot land," that is, the lowlands.

tierra fría: "cold land," that is, the highlands.

tostada: a tortilla toasted over the fire until it is crisp.

totic: God the Father.

Tzotzil: the language spoken by the Chamulas.

yajualtiquil: a village elder who serves as an advisor to the religious and political authorities.